Green Day

Green Day

A Musical Biography

Kjersti Egerdahl

THE STORY OF THE BAND

GREENWOOD PRESS

An Imprint of ABC-CLIO, LLC

A B C 🔻 C L I O

Santa Barbara, California • Denver, Colorado • Oxford, England

Library of Congress Cataloging-in-Publication Data

Egerdahl, Kjersti.
   Green Day : a musical biography / Kjersti Egerdahl.
      p. cm. — (The story of the band)
   Includes index.
   ISBN 978-0-313-36597-3 (hard copy : alk. paper) — ISBN 978-0-313-36598-0 (ebook)
   1. Green Day (Musical group). 2. Punk rock musicians—United States—Biography.
I. Title.
   ML421.G74E44   2010
   [B] 782.42166092'2—dc22   2009042079

14 13 12 11 10   1 2 3 4 5

This book is also available on the World Wide Web as an eBook.

Visit www.abc-clio.com for details.

ABC-CLIO, LLC
130 Cremona Drive, P.O. Box 1911
Santa Barbara, California 93116-1911

This book is printed on acid-free paper ∞

Manufactured in the United States of America

Contents

Photo essay follows page 90

Series Foreword

Green Day! The Beatles! U2! The Rolling Stones! These are just a few of the many bands that have shaped our lives. Written for high school students and general readers, each volume in this exciting series traces the life of a band from its beginning to the present day. Each examines the early life and family of band members, their formative years, their inspirations, their career preparation and training, and the band's awards, achievements, and lasting contributions to music.

Designed to foster student research, the series has a convenient format. Each book begins with a timeline that charts the major events in the life of the band. The narrative chapters that follow trace the birth, growth, and lasting influence of the band across time. Appendices highlight awards and other accomplishments, and a selected bibliography lists the most important print and electronic resources for high school student research-or for anyone just interested in learning more about the band.

These books also help students learn about social history. Music, perhaps more than any other force, has shaped our culture, especially in recent times. Songs comment on the events of their era and capture the spirit of their age. They powerfully touch the lives of listeners and help people-especially young people-define who they are. So too, the lifestyles of band members reflect larger social trends and promote and provoke reactions within society. By learning about the bands, students also learn more about the world they live in.

So have a seat, settle in, and crank up the volume!

Timeline

February 17, 1972	Billie Joe Armstrong born in Oakland.
May 4, 1972	Michael Ryan Pritchard (later Mike Dirnt) born in Oakland and adopted six weeks later.
December 9, 1972	Frank Edwin Wright III (later Tré Cool) born in Mendocino County.
September 1, 1982	Armstrong's father, Andy, dies.
1983	Dirnt and Armstrong meet at Carquinez Middle School at age eleven.
1985	Larry Livermore forms the Lookouts with Tré Cool on drums.
December 31, 1986	924 Gilman Street opens.
1987	Dirnt moves in with the Armstrong family at age fifteen.
April 1987	Operation Ivy forms around the same time that Dirnt and Armstrong start going to shows at 924 Gilman.

November 26, 1988	Sweet Children plays its first show at 924 Gilman, with John Kiffmeyer on drums.
Early 1989	Larry Livermore signs Sweet Children to Lookout! Records.
May 28, 1989	Operation Ivy's last show, and Sweet Children's first show under the name Green Day.
April 1989	Lookout! releases the *1,000 Hours* EP.
Spring 1990	Lookout! releases the *Slappy* EP.
Summer/Fall 1990	Lookout! releases *39/Smooth*, Green Day's first LP.
June 1990	Green Day leaves on its first tour.
July 1990	The Lookouts break up.
November 1990	Tré Cool plays drums with Green Day for the first time; Kiffmeyer is ousted.
1991	Green Day's first tour with Tré Cool on drums.
November 1991 -February 1992	Green Day's first European tour.
January 17, 1992	Lookout! releases *Kerplunk!*
August 1993	Green Day signs to Reprise Records, a subsidiary of Warner Bros. Records.
September 24, 1993	Green Day's last show at 924 Gilman.
February 1, 1994	Reprise Records releases *Dookie*.
Summer 1994	Armstrong marries Adrienne Nesser.
August 14, 1994	Green Day's set at the Woodstock '94 festival turns into a mud fight.
July 1995	Green Day fires its managers and starts managing itself.

October 10, 1995	Reprise releases *Insomniac.*
Late 1996	Green Day cancels the European leg of its world tour, citing exhaustion.
October 14, 1997	Reprise releases *Nimrod.*
January 1998	"Good Riddance" single released, becomes a major hit.
1998	Armstrong and Adrienne form Adeline Records with friends.
October 3, 2000	Reprise releases *Minority.*
June 2001	Dirnt's adoptive mother dies of an alcohol-related illness.
November 13, 2001	Reprise releases the compilation *International Superhits.*
Spring 2002	Green Day plays the Pop Disaster tour with upstart punks Blink-182.
July 2002	Reprise releases the compilation of B-sides *Shenanigans.*
November 2002	The master recordings of *Cigarettes and Valentines* are lost or stolen and the band starts over from scratch.
September 2003	Adeline releases the Network's album *Money Money 20/20.* It is not a Green Day album.
September 21, 2004	Reprise releases *American Idiot.*
February 13, 2005	*American Idiot* wins the Grammy for Best Rock Album.
November 15, 2005	Reprise releases the CD/DVD *Bullet in a Bible.*
August 25, 2005	Green Day takes back the rights to its early albums from Lookout! after the label fails to pay royalties.

September 2006   Green Day and U2 collaborate on a recording
                          of "The Saints Are Coming" as a benefit for
                          Hurricane Katrina victims.

December 19, 2006   Lookout! albums reissued by Reprise.

June 12, 2007   Green Day covers John Lennon's "Working
                          Class Hero" for the benefit album *Instant
                          Karma: The Amnesty International Campaign to
                          Save Darfur*.

May 20, 2008   Jingletown Records (a subsidiary of Warner
                          Bros.) releases the Foxboro Hot Tubs's album
                          Stop Drop and Roll!!! Like the Network's
                          Money Money 20/20, it is not a Green Day
                          album.

May 15, 2009   Reprise releases *21st Century Breakdown*.

July 3, 2009   Green Day's two-year world tour kicks off in
                          Seattle.

September 4, 2009   The musical adapted from *American Idiot*
                          opens at the Berkeley Repertory Theater.

CHAPTER ONE

Sweet Children

Most people experience Rodeo, California from the freeway, when the steady stream of suburban houses gives way to the towers and massive containers of an oil refinery on the shores of San Francisco Bay. Most people don't stop: they're either driving north toward the exclusive wineries and resorts of Napa Valley, twenty-five miles away, or south toward the countercultural outpost of Berkeley, just fifteen miles away. For Billie Joe Armstrong and Mike Dirnt, the founding members of Green Day, Berkeley would prove far more influential than Napa, but the first years of their lives took shape in the shadow of the refinery, in the town that, years later, inspired the song "Jesus of Suburbia." The city is so close—Berkeley and San Francisco are both outposts of art, music, and independent thinking—but options in the suburbs are so limited. As Armstrong later said about the song, "It's that lost feeling. Hanging out at the 7–Eleven. Disenfranchised. Alienated. You just get that feeling of 'I've got to get out of here. There's more to life than this town.'"[1] That feeling is part of what makes their music so accessible: they know what it's like to feel trapped in your own hometown, something many of their listeners have experienced. Rodeo might even be a little worse than the suburban wastelands where many fans grew up, given the refinery. Armstrong remembers kids at his elementary school getting sent home with headaches, and the city sometimes warned citizens to shut all their doors and windows if something unhealthy was blowing in from the refinery. In Rodeo, even the air is something to escape from.

The town wasn't always a wasteland. For Armstrong's parents, Andy (a truck driver) and Ollie (a waitress), it was a place where they could afford their own home and raise a large family on lower-middle-class paychecks. Ollie was one of twelve children in her family, who all moved out from Oklahoma during World War II so her parents could find work in the Richmond shipyards. She married her first husband at just nineteen, and divorced in her early twenties after her son Alan was born, working all the while as a waitress. She has fond memories of serving members of the notorious motorcycle gang at Mel's Drive-In in Berkeley. "We'd wait on the Hells Angels. They were so good to us." No wonder she calls that gig "the best job in the world."[2] After her brief first marriage, she met Andy Armstrong at a Slim Slaughter show at the Melody Club in Albany. He was a big man and a former boxer who played the drums and loved jazz almost as much as Ollie loved country. He grew up in Berkeley as one of eight siblings, and together he and Ollie raised six children.

Billie Joe was the youngest of the Armstrong clan, born February 17, 1972, at an Oakland hospital when his mother was forty years old. An adorable, curly-haired child, he was not born with the name William Joseph Armstrong, as one might suspect—perhaps his mother's love of country music had an influence there. His oldest brother, Alan, was twenty-two and had already moved out of the house, so Billie Joe and David shared one bedroom and the three girls, Marci, Holly, and Anna, shared another room. Aside from the normal fighting of kids in close quarters, the family was comfortable and never had trouble making a living. Ollie continued working part-time as a waitress at Rod's Hickory Pit in nearby Vallejo while raising the kids, and Andy worked steadily driving Safeway trucks, and worked the occasional overnight job.

THE FIRST SONGS

The Armstrong house always had some kind of music around, whether it was the boys banging on the drum set that Andy kept in the living room, or Ollie's collection of country albums by greats like Hank Williams, Patsy Cline, and Willie Nelson. Armstrong always had a cheap, old nylon-string guitar around to play with as well. When he was only five, Ollie decided to sign him and some of his siblings up for piano lessons, and took them down to Fiatarone's in Pinole, the local music shop owned by James and Marie-Louise Fiatarone. When Armstrong came in with his mother, Marie-Louise took him to the back room and had him sing the children's song "He's Got the Whole World in His Hands." She was shocked by his ability to pay attention and sing right on pitch. His proud mother signed him up for weekly piano and voice lessons on the spot.

To help cover what would have been a major expense for the large family, the Fiatarones offered to have Armstrong record a single for their in-house label, Fiat Records. They had written a cute, simple song called "Look for Love," and took Armstrong to Fantasy Studios in Berkeley to record—the same building in which he would record *Dookie* sixteen years later. Marie-Louise Fiatarone played keyboards, and their son Jim played guitar. Marie-Louise interviews Armstrong on the B-side of this rare single, a track titled "Meet Billie Joe," which is sampled at the beginning of Green Day's 2001 album, *International Superhits*. "Billie Joe, it's certainly exciting to meet you here at the recording studio right after you've just made your very first record," Marie-Louise says. "How does it feel?" Billie Joe pauses a moment, then chirps, "Hmm…wonderful!"[3] His mother still cherishes her copy of "Look for Love," which could bring in some serious cash on eBay today: only 800 copies of the 7-inch single were ever created. As a result of that first recording, he got some good press when the local paper printed an item titled "Billie Joe Armstrong, 5, Might Be on His Way to the Top."

As a next step, the Fiatarones helped him enter local competitions. He also sang in children's hospitals and retirement homes occasionally, with his dad on drums and the Fiatarones covering the other instruments. Richard Cotton, the owner of Rod's Hickory Pit, remembers Armstrong singing for seniors in the banquet room, and saw greatness in him even then. As Cotton explains, "I told Ollie, 'I'm going to see this kid's name in lights one day.'"[4] Armstrong and the Fiatarones favored standards and Broadway tunes. "'New York, New York,' you should've heard him sing that," his mother reminisces.[5] Granted, it doesn't seem very punk rock to tour small towns with your dad and sing show tunes, but it taught Armstrong how to be a showman. "I learned a lot about how to be onstage," he remembers.[6] When he was seven, his parents bought him a red Hohner guitar, and he learned to love playing as quickly as he'd learned to love singing. At age nine, he had another formative musical experience: seeing groundbreaking punks, the Ramones, in the film *Rock 'n' Roll High School*. Catchy, driving songs like "Blitzkrieg Bop" and "Pinhead" embedded themselves in his brain, and very likely formed a base for the melodic punk songs he would begin to write in just a few years.

A FAMILY CRUMBLES

A happy, productive childhood wasn't what ultimately sparked his songwriting, though. The Armstrong family, and especially the sheltered youngest, Billie Joe, sailed into rougher waters when Andy Armstrong, then only fifty-one, told his family that he had esophageal cancer. He died four months later on September 1, 1982, when Billie Joe was only ten. "My dad said on his deathbed, 'Make sure you take care of Billie Joe,'" says his brother David. "'Cause he was the youngest. And the creative one."[7]

Andy's death marked a turning point for everyone. "Our family changed a lot because my parents had been very kid oriented," Anna remembers. "And all of a sudden, my mother withdrew and threw herself into waitressing. The family structure broke up."[8] By staying busy, Ollie dealt with the loss in her own way, but her children were left to their own devices. "We didn't necessarily know how to be with each other during that time," says Anna. "We didn't know how to help each other, or support each other, because it was all just so foreign and strange."[9] Ollie's own words reflect some of the helplessness she must have felt. "All these stories about [Billie Joe] coming from a dysfunctional family, that he was from a broken home," she says. "How do you stop someone from dying?"[10] With four children still living at home (Alan and Marci, the oldest, were on their own), and left with no real savings, she didn't have much choice but to bury herself in work, moving to full-time hours at Rod's Hickory Pit. She eventually remarried, choosing a stepfather with whom none of her children grew very close.

As a result of all this upheaval, Marci says, the three youngest were spared some of the discipline that the older kids endured. Billie Joe agrees, saying, "I'm the epitome of a latchkey kid. By the time my mom, who had me when she was forty, got around to raising me, she was like, 'You do what you want, I'm sick of being strict all the time.'"[11]

ARMSTRONG'S ESCAPE

What Billie Joe Armstrong wanted to do was to lose himself in music. He got a lot of it from MTV, which had launched in 1981 and worked its way into suburban homes across California. He didn't stop at watching videos, though. His mother was somehow able to continue his music lessons, sending him to local teacher George Cole. Armstrong was less interested in learning to read music than in learning songs from his oldest brother Alan's Beatles records, which he could play by ear with surprising accuracy. He also tuned in to heavier, swaggering bands like Van Halen, Def Leppard, and Ozzy Osbourne, thanks to two slightly older boys, brothers Matt and Eric, who spent weekends at their father's house across the street. When Armstrong brought Van Halen's 1982 album *Diver Down* to a lesson with Cole, the teacher showed him a variation of the legendary Eddie Van Halen's hammer technique. The two jammed together, the student on his red Hohner and the teacher on a powder-blue Fernandez Stratocaster, a copy of Jimi Hendrix's preferred Fender Stratocaster. Armstrong looked up to Cole and idolized his guitar, which he called "Blue." Ollie saw how excited Armstrong was about his lessons, and how much he talked about "Blue," and she managed to scrape together three or four hundred dollars to buy the guitar from Cole as an early Christmas present for her son. He used "Blue" for years after that, until it was held together by nothing more than duct tape—and when it finally fell apart, he had replicas made.

When Matt and Eric's tastes began to stray from Van Halen, Armstrong went along for the ride. They passed on faster, spikier songs from bands like TSOL, from Orange County, California, and the Dead Kennedys, from San Francisco—and, of course, British punk pioneers the Sex Pistols. This was punk rock, even more dangerous than the Ramones, and it stuck with Armstrong. "I liked the rebellion and the style—those guys reminded me of gangsters," he says.[12] When it came to discovering and playing new music, Armstrong was about to meet his match.

PARTNERS IN CRIME

Michael Ryan Pritchard, later to be known as Mike Dirnt, was an accident-prone eleven-year-old boy with a goofy grin when he met Armstrong at Carquinez Middle School. "At first we didn't like each other," admits Dirnt, "because we were both class clowns."[13] After a short period of standoffishness, the two bonded over music and spent every lunch period together, talking about Van Halen and the darker stuff Pritchard liked: Judas Priest and Iron Maiden. They had more than just music in common; both had been marked by loss and change at a young age. Pritchard was born in Oakland on May 4, 1972, to a heroin-addicted Native American woman who gave him up for adoption. Perhaps as a result of her addiction, he suffered periodic illnesses that caused him to miss school throughout his childhood. At six weeks old, he was placed with foster parents in El Sobrante, near Rodeo. The young couple, Cheryl Nasser and Patrick Pritchard, raised him and his sister Mycla until their relationship deteriorated and one verbal fight resulted in a call to the police. Cheryl moved out and took Mycla to live in Rodeo, and Pritchard soon followed them. Where he had previously been a fearless kid who did well in school, he became sullen and withdrawn. "There were all sorts of things happening," he remembers. "When I was in fourth or fifth grade, my mom stayed out all night, came home the next day with a guy, and he moved in. I'd never met the guy before, and all of a sudden he's my stepdad. We didn't get along for years."[14] With both friends itching to escape the unwanted authority of their stepfathers and deal with the confusion in their lives, they accepted each other without judgment and dealt with their situations through music.

Pritchard had never owned a guitar or taken lessons, because his family was in an even tighter money situation than Armstrong's, but he wanted to play. "One day Billie had Mike over," remembers David Armstrong, "and me and my buddies were about to go out for the night and we saw them sitting on me and Billie's beds. . . . One was sitting on one side, and one was on the other. Billie was teaching Mike chords. That was about six o'clock. I got home at two o'clock in the morning, and they were still there. And Billie looked up at me and said, 'Hey, Dave, watch what Mike can do.' And Mike knew four or five songs from start to end. That's the connection they had. I don't think Mike knew a note at the beginning of the night."[15]

Through the rest of middle school, the two budding punks practiced constantly. "There was a sense of freedom where no one is looking at you and no one is critiquing what you're doing," says Armstrong. "And you don't have to better what you've done in the past because you don't have any past. It's the very beginning and you're just listening to everything for the first time and saying like 'Wow, look what I can do! Jesus Christ. Where the f*** is this coming from?'"[16]

In ninth grade, Pritchard moved on to Salesians High School in Richmond, an all-boys Catholic high school, and Armstrong followed his long line of brothers and sisters to John Swett High School, a 400-student school in Crockett. He hadn't ruled out sports as un-punk yet, having played tailback in little league football before high school, but even at his small high school he only made water boy.

PLAYING IN THE BAND

Music remained Armstrong's focus, with the Who and the Kinks, and particularly Generation X's street-fighting song "Kiss Me Deadly," making an impression with their combined melody and power. Of "Kiss Me Deadly," Armstrong says, "It embodied passion and rebellion. It was punk rock, but at the same time it was really sweet, too. Generation X was the very first punk band I ever got into and that song was instrumental in me wanting to start a band."[17] Soon Armstrong, Pritchard, and friends Jason Relva and Sean Hughes had formed a loose music-making unit—they weren't quite a band yet, but they were making a lot of noise. When they were playing a lot of metal songs, they called themselves Condom; after they switched to a more rock sound, they went with Desecrated Youth. Taking advantage of Ollie's long hours, they set up their instruments in the Armstrongs' living room. It was all fun, but for Armstrong it was something more. He emerged as the lead guitarist and default band leader, suggesting to Hughes that he pick up the bass and write songs for the band to learn. Mike was on rhythm guitar at this point, with Raj Punjabi stopping by occasionally to play drums, and Jason Relva stepping in where they needed him and playing the part of the audience. Relva's friendship meant a lot to Pritchard and Armstrong, and it was his unexpected death in a car accident in 1992 at only nineteen that inspired their 1995 punk anthem, "J.A.R."

Pritchard and Hughes transferred to Pinole Valley High school, a much bigger and more diverse public school, and, in eleventh grade, Armstrong used his brother Alan's address to switch schools and join them. In 1986, it wasn't as easy to walk around looking like a greasy rocker as it is now. Their group of friends got hassled by bullies, who they labeled "Pods" (Pinole Oriented Dicks). Needless to say, they didn't have girlfriends.

But they did have a band, and it finally had a name. They decided to call themselves Sweet Children, which was the title of one of Armstrong's earliest songs. Robert Brown, a classmate at Pinole, remembers them bugging him to come listen to them play, and he finally went when they played at school for Foreign Foods Day. "They had exotic food and a couple of bands play," he says. "Sweet Children were one of them. They all played in the quad. Out in the middle of the school. I remember liking them. But most of the people that were really paying attention to them were the other few punks at our school. The jocks and everyone else didn't care."[18]

Sweet Children were fast moving beyond "the jocks and everyone else." Thanks to his older sister Anna, Armstrong got deeper into college rock, mid-'80s alternative music like Hüsker Dü and Camper Van Beethoven. The Replacements hit home with him, and he taught himself and then the rest of Sweet Children their song "If Only You Were Lonely." Anna took him to an R.E.M. show in Santa Cruz, south of San Francisco, that made a big impact on the young songwriter. "Michael Stipe had a shaved head and wore an old overcoat," Armstrong remembers. "I thought, 'This is different.'"[19] He met some other punks at that show who pushed him up to the front of the stage, and he started to sense that there might be a community for him in punk rock. Soon, he and Pritchard would fully embrace punk rock as a life—but, first, they had to deal with their own lives.

Pritchard's family situation continued to be rough. His mother was having money troubles, so he got a job as a cook at The Nantucket, a seafood restaurant in Crockett. This wasn't enough to solve their problems, though, and his mother decided to take Mike and his sister and leave Rodeo, without their stepfather. Rather than break up the band and switch high schools just as their junior year was starting, Pritchard and Armstrong came up with a plan: Armstrong asked his mother if Pritchard could stay with them for a while. Ollie liked Pritchard, who was always respectful around her, and so the two close friends became even more like brothers. Pritchard also became closer with his stepfather, something of a surprise, considering the fact that they had never gotten along very well before. "He instilled a lot in me," Pritchard remembers. "The one thing my family did give me is blue-collar morals. But then he died when I was 17."[20] Pritchard's sister opted out of the whole mess, leaving home at thirteen. Despite all this loss and change, the self-motivated Pritchard kept passing his classes and working (and smelling like fish), all the while plotting with Armstrong and Hughes how to get Sweet Children going.

They got their first real clue as to where their music could take them in a conversation with a guy around their age called Eggplant. He had been hanging out in Berkeley, and he had heard and seen the new punk movement that was forming around 924 Gilman Street, a dank warehouse that hosted all-ages punk rock shows every weekend with the goal of challenging its patrons to expand their way of thinking as well as their musical taste. "He was from Pinole," remembers Hughes, "and his sister Phaedra was friends with my sister, so he was over one night and Billie and Mike happened to be there and he was talking about Gilman and these great bands like Isocracy and how we should check it out. Billie was more intrigued by it than I was at first. He really held an ear to him that night."[21]

MIRACLE ON GILMAN STREET

924 Gilman Street began as the brainchild of Tim Yohannan, one of the Bay Area's punk elders, who had been a war protester in the 1960s and was inspired again by the rise of punk in the 1970s. He hosted a punk rock radio show called Maximumrocknroll that played intense new bands like Black Flag, the Germs, and the Dead Kennedys; punks in the Bay Area taped the show and shared the tapes with distant friends, and it was eventually syndicated. Based on the success of the radio show, Yohannan started a zine of the same name, an independent, underground publication that covered punk rock and radical-left political life via reviews, interviews, and the avidly read scene reports from cities around the world. When he had saved up enough cash, Yohannan put a long-term plan into action: he wanted the Bay Area to have a permanent punk outpost, a center for a community that shared do-it-yourself values and independent thinking, with no racism, sexism, or homophobia from the music or the audience.

There were always punk shows in the Bay Area, but the venues popped up and vanished regularly, and the shows were often plagued by violence. The standard procedure was to find an abandoned building or under-used pizza joint and host shows there until the cops caught wind of it and shut the place down. As a result, it was hard for new bands (like Sweet Children) to get a foothold in a constantly changing scene. Yohannan wanted this to change; he wanted a club that could be a permanent center for punk rockers. "Tim's whole thing was, 'We're gonna create this club and it's going to be solid. Totally cool with the city, all the right permits, drug- and alcohol-free place," says Jesse Michaels, who became the frontman for one of Gilman's standout bands, Operation Ivy.[22] From the start, Yohannan and his collaborators (people who booked shows, created zines, or played music) knew that the club would have to be all-ages and eliminate alcohol. The red tape from the city, the notice from the cops, and the exclusion of teenagers, one of punk's main audiences, would have hobbled the club from the beginning.

A local punk rocker who regularly booked underground shows found a location for the club at number 924 on a run-down stretch of Gilman Street, in the warehouse of a chair-caning company. Taking the next step, Yohannan and company advertised their ideas for the club through flyers, *Maximumrocknroll*, and the MRR radio show, collecting a team of devoted volunteers. "We were completely oblivious about what we were about to go through, which was eight months of paying rent on the place before we could even open, and investing over $40,000 in the place for rent, construction, etc., also before we could open," remembers Tim Yohannan.[23] This band of punk rockers came together and knocked on the doors of the other small businesses throughout the neighborhood, explaining their goal of a youth community center (with music), and showing that they were organized. When construction began to remodel the warehouse, they had endless inspections and spoke before the zoning board of the city. They did enjoy the added advantage that Berkeley has been known as a center of counterculture and alternative living since at least the 1950s, and city officials, including the mayor, were generally supportive. Yohannan had also done a lot of precinct organizing and other election work in Berkeley, so he knew who to call in city government and asked them to cast their votes for Gilman.

Even the building owner was helpful and wanted the club to succeed—possibly because the warehouse had stood empty for so long and the neighborhood wasn't exactly a hotspot. "My father owned the building at the time," remembers Jim Widess, "and he had no problem with all the delays and red tape that were encountered with the city once MRR and Co. came into the space and tried to open the club. He was a very generous person—he surprised me with his generosity toward the club, like reduced rent before it actually opened, things like that."[24]

Yohannan wanted the club to feel like a clubhouse, so that people would feel ownership and responsibility and want to keep the music coming. He started the membership policy where everyone had to throw in a dollar or two for the club each year and, theoretically, attend Sunday afternoon committee meetings as a way of controlling the violence that often broke out at punk shows at that time. The extra income ended up making a huge difference to the club's survival in the years to come.

A PUNK CLUB RUN BY PUNKS

The final approval from the city came on the afternoon before their first show: New Year's Eve, December 1986. The first bands on the soon-to-be-legendary stage were Impulse Manslaughter, Christ on Parade, Silkworms, AMQA, and Soup. Tim Armstrong, who would soon join Operation Ivy, and later, Rancid, was there that first night. He recalls, "I felt at home as soon as I walked into the place. There was no backstage. It was a punk club run by punks. There was no sense of hierarchy at all. Things were equal. I was overwhelmed. It was as exciting as the first time I picked up a Ramones album. I felt something magical was happening again, but this time I was in the middle of it."[25] After more than twenty years, Gilman is still in the same location, on a dirty street in a backwater neighborhood, and it still has four or five bands per night every weekend. Shows are still under $10, and punks of all ages (mostly young) still crowd the floor. "It has worthy and yet modest goals," Avengers member Penelope Houston told the zine *Punk Planet*. She notes, "They're not trying to change the world, but rather just change the world for themselves. To have a place to play; to have a place to meet; to provide a space for their own community."[26]

In this politically charged atmosphere, sharp, aware punk rock took off. It was occasionally self-serious and overly politically correct (there were endless meetings to come up with a non-coercive approach to security), but many bands flourished that would otherwise have been choked out in the violent hardcore scene. Gilman didn't end the fighting at other clubs (and skinheads did occasionally try to start brawls at Gilman) but it did take the pressure off of punks to seem hard and cool. Everyone wanted to see what they could get away with in such a new environment. Lawrence Livermore, a *Maximumrocknroll* columnist who went on to found Lookout! Records, was quoted in the local paper when the club opened. "Even though punk has originally been involved with negativity and darkness, it's becoming brighter," he said.[27]

HOME AWAY FROM HOME

For Armstrong and Pritchard, Gilman was the light at the end of the tunnel. "It saved me from living in a refinery town all my life," Armstrong told *Spin* in 1995. "Everything that I have now pretty much branched from that whole scene."[28] The two decidedly unmacho punks volunteered as security guards in exchange for free tickets to shows at Gilman. "We lived and died for that place," remembers Pritchard. "At the time, it meant everything."[29] They were exposed to all kinds of new ideas at the world of Gilman Street, from new ways of putting together a band, to vegetarianism, socialism, and the many sins of Ronald Reagan, the Republican president at the time.

They were also exposed to a new kind of girl, the kind that might actually think guitar skills were attractive. Armstrong met his first real girlfriend, Arica Paleno, at Gilman. "I'm fascinated and attracted to talent, and that's what it was for me," Paleno says of Armstrong. "Because nobody thought he was a super hot guy at sixteen, that's for sure."[30] The song "Christie Road," on Green Day's second full-length album, *Kerplunk!*, was written about Paleno, who was always grounded and sneaking out of the house to meet Armstrong. She kept the lyric book where Armstrong first wrote down the words to that and other early songs.

The girls and the goofiness were enough to motivate Armstrong and Pritchard (and likely many others) to stick it out at Gilman despite the endless socialist-style meetings and debates on points like "Should we have advertising for shows at all?" and "Should bands be required to work at the club in order to play?" Get past all the restrictions and guidelines, though, and it was easy to see the reason this club became legendary and inspired countless bands to form: people wanted their own place, on their own terms, and made it happen. Jesse Michaels of Operation Ivy spelled it out in *Maximumrocknroll*, saying that, "instead of saying THEY don't allow smoking in this room or whatever, and people go there they say THEY meaning some mysterious higher-up at the club or whatever, I'd like to hear people saying WE."[31] For the most part, that's what happened. The club survived its most precarious situation early on, when *Maximumrocknroll* pulled out on September 12, 1988, about a year after the club had opened. Aaron Cometbus (Aaron Elliot) analyzed the transition in a limited edition, ten-year anniversary issue of his zine *Cometbus*. He wrote, "Tim [Yohannan] took on a paternal role at Gilman, and got all the problems that came with being a parent. Yes, he had supported us and guided us, and it was a thankless job. But like all parents, he lectured us to be more responsible, but didn't seem willing to give up any of his own authority."[32] By October 20, a new foundation called the Alternative Music Foundation was officially incorporated with the city, and took over running the club—but no one ever called it by that name. It was always Gilman.

OPERATION IVY

This transitional year, 1988, saw a lot of growth that would affect Armstrong's and Dirnt's futures. There was Armstrong's first girlfriend, of course, and the changes at Gilman, but a new band also came on the scene that would inspire Sweet Children to climb to the next level by the end of the year. In the spring of 1988, guitarist Tim "Lint" Armstrong and bassist Matt "McCall" Freeman (Lint gave him the nickname in honor of the late-'80s crime show *The Equalizer*) hadn't played music since their ska band Basic Radio broke up, but found their missing links in singer Jesse Michaels and drummer Dave Mello. Together, they formed one of the most influential bands to come out of Gilman, although not the best-selling: Operation Ivy.

Armstrong felt the charisma and strength in their melodic, light speed blend of ska, reggae, and punk. People could dance to it, and every show was a celebration. They acted on their ideals of inclusiveness and unity as well: when Armstrong went to see Operation Ivy for the first time at age fifteen, he couldn't get in because he was underage. But one of the band members heard that he had been turned away, and brought him inside to see the show. It made a lasting impression and showed how accessible the bands at Gilman wanted to be. Their positive politics backed up their sing-along melodies, and the taste-enforcers at *Maximumrocknroll* even praised the band's EP, *Hectic*, for being catchy: "Straight up—this is a must!"[33] The album and the scrappy tours that ensued spread the word about Gilman Street around the country and helped lay the groundwork for Green Day's eventual rise—after all, their connection to the Gilman scene won them instant credibility in far-flung punk communities.

Hectic came out on Lookout! Records, the label started by thirty-something punk Larry Livermore of rural Mendocino County. It was inspired by his zine of the same name, which covered East Bay music as well as local news and politics. Lookout! was having a great year: in the first month of 1988, Livermore released four EPs by Crimpshrine, Isocracy, Corrupted Morals, and Operation Ivy, all stalwarts of the Gilman scene. He started the label mainly to release an album by his own semi-talented band called, naturally, the Lookouts. The band started sometime in 1985, and featured a twelve-year-old drummer called Tré Cool, who would eventually become a key part of Armstrong and Pritchard's lives.

BECOMING COOL

Tré Cool, born Frank Edwin Wright III on December 9, 1972, grew up in Willits, California, a tiny mountain town in Mendocino County. His father, Frank Wright II, was a helicopter pilot in Vietnam, and decided to move to the country after the war, heading to the mountains of Mendocino with his wife, Linda, and their two children. "It was mind-numbing," says Cool. "I'd walk around this huge mountain. It was complete wilderness."[34] It was hippie country, known for its marijuana crops and ties to the Grateful Dead, and the Wright family lived off the grid, with no electricity or running water. To entertain himself, the young Cool pounded on things: rocks, bicycles, tree stumps. His goofball antics and hyperactive sense of humor most likely stem from his early attempts to deal with his father's dark postwar mentality. Music, for him, also provided an escape from a moody father and a lonely setting.

The nearest neighbor was a mile away, but, luckily, that neighbor was Larry Livermore. Livermore's girlfriend, who had played drums with him, had recently left him, and so, to keep his dreams of forming a band alive, he recruited Cool to play drums in the Lookouts, and another neighborhood kid, fourteen-year-old Kain Kong, to play bass. None of them knew how to play, but that didn't seem like an obstacle. "One of the greatest (and, some say, worst) legacies of the punk movement was that anyone can be in a band," Livermore says. "Even me, as it turned out. When I formed [that band] I quickly became the laughing stock of the remote mountain community. . . ."[35] Punk hadn't exactly found an audience among the Grateful Dead–loving hippies in Mendocino. But it had a true devotee in Cool. The kid had such charm and enthusiasm that Livermore overlooked his loud, sometimes bratty, behavior, and let him bash away on a drum set that a friend had left behind after moving to Brazil. Cool's instinct for thrashing on the drums was so strong that Livermore had to take the cymbals off the drum set, lock them in a cupboard, and return them one at a time over the next several weeks as Cool learned to control his decibel levels. Around the same time, Livermore gave him his nickname, and he has since legally changed his name to Tré Cool (as in *trés* cool, French for *very cool*). At the time, nobody questioned Livermore for spending his free time with two young neighborhood kids. "I just think that because he had a youthful spirit, [Tré] and everyone else was really comfortable about it," says Wendy Norris, one of Cool's childhood friends. "It wasn't like he was this lonely old guy who hung around with little boys."[36]

The Lookouts soon began playing shows "off the mountain," and Cool's horizons expanded. The high school band teacher enlisted the sixth-grader to play in the high school jazz band, even picking him up and driving him to practice, since he was the only student who could understand the music. Despite being elected class president one year in high school, the charismatic Cool got his GED at sixteen and left school to concentrate on punk rock. The Lookouts were soon playing Gilman as well as warehouses and parties all over the East Bay.

ENTER AL SOBRANTE

Sweet Children had yet to achieve the same success: Tim Yohannan had dismissed them as "not punk enough."[37] They knew Cool enough to say hi, but never hung out. Their fortunes changed when they met John Kiffmeyer from El Sobrante, who went by the stage name Al Sobrante. Four years older than Armstrong and Pritchard, he was already the drummer for the established band Isocracy, named after a system of government where all the people share equal power.

They'd been playing Gilman almost since the beginning, and with a name like that, it's no surprise that they were often referred to as the "house band." They were famous for throwing garbage everywhere throughout their set, until the whole floor was covered in junk from stuffed animals to dirty diapers to candy.

The writers at *Maximumrocknroll* were fans of Isocracy's music and their humor as well. So when Kiffmeyer joined as Sweet Children's drummer, he gave them instant credibility. "There was a certain kind of social hierarchy, and all these people were really young in the Berkeley Gilman scene," says Chris Appelgren, who was sixteen at the time but went on to be president of Lookout! Records. Appelgren explained, "John took Sweet Children from being these kind of kids who maybe sort of hung out at Gilman the same way a lot of us did to actually being a real part of the scene."[38] Kiffmeyer shared his expertise about booking shows and touring, but he also took over the leadership role from Armstrong. For the time being, that was OK with Armstrong, Pritchard, and Hughes—the band just needed to get a foot in the door.

They finally landed a spot on a Gilman Street bill, opening for Neurosis over Thanksgiving weekend in 1988. As a warm-up, they played their first show with Kiffmeyer at Rod's Hickory Pit, attended mostly by Armstrong's big family. The Gilman show was well-received, and included originals like "Sweet Children," "Strangeland," and "The Best Thing in Town," the first song Armstrong and Pritchard co-wrote, as well as covers like "Johnny B. Goode" and The Who's "My Generation." They didn't have a lot of style, but they could play, and that made an impression. "Compared with a lot of bands, they sort of made an instant name for themselves because everyone was surprised by how young they were," remembers Jeff Ott of Crimpshrine. "And because their music was on the polished side. They sang harmony, which was totally unusual."[39]

Sweet Children got organized and lined up a bunch of house party slots to follow their Gilman debut. They also became a trio. Bassist Sean Hughes left Sweet Children soon after Kiffmeyer came on board and the band started getting more gigs. Also, Pritchard switched from rhythm guitar to bass. "I took lessons, but I never practiced," says Hughes, "They were gunning to switch up anyway, and I just dropped out. By then, they were really organized. They were definitely cruising."[40] Pritchard learned bass even faster than he had learned guitar, carrying his instrument to school and practicing at lunch and during breaks. The familiar sound of him plucking the strings on his unamplified bass, "*dirnt, dirnt, dirnt,*" became something of a joke among his friends and classmates, and they started calling him Mike Dirnt.[41] He took the name as a source of pride, and was known forever after as Mike Dirnt.

With all these pieces in place, the band played anywhere they could. Because two-thirds of the band was still five years underage, the normal circuit of bars and clubs was out. Sweet Children solidified their reputation at house parties, however, and eventually caught the attention of Larry Livermore at one of them. They drove out to Willits and played a house show powered only by a generator, as there wasn't any other source of power. Only about five kids showed up. Nevertheless, Livermore says, "As I've often said, they played for those five kids as if they were the Beatles at Shea Stadium, and just as with Op Ivy, I knew before they finished their first song that I wanted to do their record."[42] Lookout! had accumulated some cash and some credibility with the local success of Operation Ivy's *Hectic* EP, so he was ready to take on Sweet Children, despite low expectations of how a record by a young, relatively pop-oriented band would sell. If only for the sake of documenting what was going on at the time, a record deal with Lookout! was the logical next step for a band that already had a polished signature sound and a following at Gilman Street.

NOTES

1. Marc Spitz, *Nobody Likes You: Inside the Turbulent Life, Times, and Music of Green Day* (New York: Hyperion, 2006), 2.
2. Tony Hicks, "Son's on a roll, but mom's the rock: Green Day frontman's success has not spoiled his mother, who holds family together and—at 75—still loves work as a waitress," *Contra Costa Times*, May 13, 2007, Living section.
3. Ben Myers, *Green Day: American Idiots and the New Punk Explosion.* (New York: The Disinformation Company, Inc. 2006), 18.
4. Ibid., 18.
5. Hicks, Living section.
6. Spitz, 8.
7. Ibid., 9.
8. Chris Mundy, "Green Daze," *Rolling Stone*, January 26, 1995, 38.
9. Spitz, 10.

10. Hicks, Living section.
11. Craig Marks, "An American Family," *Spin*, December 1995, 61.
12. Myers, 22.
13. Marks, 61.
14. Mundy, 38.
15. Spitz, 13-14.
16. Ibid., 14.
17. Myers, 26.
18. Spitz, 18.
19. Ibid., 18.
20. Mundy, 38.
21. Spitz, 20.
22. Ibid., 31.
23. Brian Edge, *924 Gilman: The Story So Far* (San Francisco: Maximumrocknroll, 2004), 7.
24. Ibid., 23.
25. Spitz, 33-34.
26. Edge, 4.
27. Carol Percy, "Project club a place to listen, stomp and celebrate," *West County Times*, March 15, 1988, 1D.
28. Marks, 138.
29. Spitz, 35.
30. Ibid., 36.
31. Brian and David, "Operation Ivy," *Maximumrocknroll*, January 1988, 10.
32. Aaron Cometbus, "Ten Years at Gilman: A Scrapbook," *Cometbus* 38 ?, January 3, 1997, 9.
33. M. S., Review of *Hectic EP*, by Operation Ivy, *Maximumrocknroll*, January 1988, 17.
34. Mundy, 39.
35. Myers, 29.
36. Spitz, 54.
37. Ibid., 42.
38. Ibid., 45.
39. Ibid., 46.
40. Ibid., 49.
41. Ibid., 50.
42. Ibid., 63.

CHAPTER TWO

Lookout!

Sweet Children headed into a local East Bay studio in early 1989 to lay down four tracks for their first EP, *1,000 Hours*. The budget was allegedly limited to $650, and everything was done after just two days in the studio. They played live, everyone in the same room, with just a few overdubs added later. Critics agree that on these earliest recordings, the sound of Green Day is already there: these young kids were lucky enough to find their voice right away.

They decided they hadn't found their name yet, though. Just before the album was scheduled to come out, the band started thinking that Sweet Children sounded a little too, well, young. Besides, there was already a band at Gilman called Sweet Baby. Billie Joe Armstrong had written a song called "Green Day," an ode to long afternoons discovering an alternate reality in your bedroom—and so the band agreed to change their name to Green Day. "I think the general feeling was that the first name wasn't a very good choice, and that the second one was better," says Jeff Ott of Gilman band Crimpshrine. "Plus, they were total potheads."[1] Drummer John Kiffmeyer wrote the name on the back of his black leather jacket, and it was official. Lookout! Records just had to deal with it. "How did I feel?" says label head Lawrence Livermore. "Well, I was just about to put out their first record and I went ballistic. I was like, 'Everybody knows you as Sweet Children. How am I supposed to sell a record by a band called Green Day?'"[2] That was the last time anyone ever asked that question.

ON THE RECORD

1,000 Hours came out in April 1989, and Lookout! had ordered up 1,200 copies of the seven-inch single in colors as wild as kids' hair at Gilman: six hundred copies on green vinyl, two hundred on purple, two hundred on red, one hundred on clear vinyl, and one hundred on yellow and blue.[3] The band pitched in willingly to help put the record together, DIY-style. "We used to go into the Lookout! office to help them fold all the sleeves for the seven-inch records," says Mike Dirnt, "Yeah, and I remember thinking, 'Man, if putting the sleeves together is this hard, then I'm f***** if I want to do the rest of the work.' That's when I realized that I probably wouldn't want to run my own label full time."[4] The sleeves were simple: the front cover just had their logo and the album title, and the back showed the band hanging out. Other than a list of song titles, the only other information was the oddball credits section: "Billy [sic]: Guitar, Hat," "Mike: Bass, Hair," and "John: Drums, Bus."

1,000 Hours sold fairly well for Lookout! and soon spread the word about this young band through the Gilman scene. In a California punk scene with its fair share of hard-line political crusty punks and stagnating hardcore bands, Green Day was the pop band it was OK to like. They couldn't completely lose the baby-faced aspects of their look and sound just by changing their name, but their sound was already polished and they were ready to work hard.

"I give 100 percent [commitment] to a song [while I'm writing it]," Armstrong says, "Even if it's 100 percent a piece of shit."[5] Fortunately, he rarely writes that type of song. Even those earliest songs showed the band's dedication to shaping each song into a finished piece. They may have been unsophisticated, but they weren't rip-offs of any other band. Armstrong later pinpointed "1,000 Hours" as his least favorite song of that time period: "Not only was it not for a band to play or to play as a band, it's just the sappiest song about a girl, to the point where it's like a bad John Hughes movie!"[6] In 1989, though, it was probably a little hard for pot-smoking couch potato teenagers to avoid John Hughes, or, say, Tiffany, whose 1988 hit "I Think We're

Alone Now" deals with confused teenage love in a similarly melodic way. That's really just another way of saying that Green Day had hit upon a nearly universal theme, even if they had yet to find the best way of expressing it.

In fact, several other punk bands around this time had gotten fed up with hardcore and started to move closer to the pop end of the spectrum. Los Angeles band Bad Religion was one of the very first bands in the '80s to start moving toward what would become pop-punk and skate-punk in the '90s. Their lyrics were undeniably political, but they mixed that with vocal harmonies. The younger band NOFX aligned with the goofy side of Gilman, and their contemporaries, such as the Offspring, brought pounding, anthemic choruses to the game. Gilman bands like Screeching Weasel, the Mr. T. Experience, Samiam, and Crimpshrine all helped break the grip of hardcore and nudge punk, however unwittingly, toward a broader audience.

The political atmosphere at Gilman, however, pervaded all the music to some extent. During President Ronald Reagan's second term in office, in the late '80s, many bands slipped a protest into their shows. "It wasn't just Reagan," longtime Gilman volunteer Jesse Townley told *Rolling Stone*. "It was an examination of the corruption of the politics of the United States, late-twentieth-century style: the quest for the almighty dollar, and the quest for conformity. You can hear that in all kinds of bands from that time and scene."[7] Dirnt says he found it impossible to hang around Gilman and stay away from politics: "It was everything from the bands we were listening to, to fanzines, to just sitting around in coffee shops or behind buildings drinking beer and talking about things with friends who had political leanings."[8] Armstrong recalls a song by Sewer Trout called "Wally and Beaver Go to Nicaragua," a song about the main characters from *Leave It to Beaver* debating U.S. intervention in Central America. "That summed up a lot of what Gilman Street was all about," he says: goofy but smart, and serious about the issues behind the songs.[9]

WELCOME TO PARADISE

Gilman lost one of its smartest, most successful bands of that time on the night Sweet Children made their debut as Green Day— May 28, 1989, was Operation Ivy's final show. The godfathers of the scene bowed out, but left Gilman in good hands: the next generation of bands was ready to take the torch being passed to them and run with it. "You could say that when Op Ivy went away, Green Day became the biggest band on the scene," says Jeff Ott of Crimp-shrine.[10]

Green Day dove in headfirst. Armstrong and Dirnt left the soft life at the Armstrong family home at seventeen. Dirnt always had a job, and usually had a place to live, but Armstrong had no use for stability. "At that age, Billie was so into music that he was distracted by the rest of his life—the rest of his life was a distraction from him doing his music," says Bill Schneider, Green Day's current road manager (at that time a member of the Gilman band Monsula). Schneider continues, "He didn't have jobs—he was so content to sleep on somebody's couch. He just waited for Mike to get a place to live and then go sleep on the couch there. He was just distracted with having to live an ordinary life."[11]

Armstrong's unshakable confidence and Dirnt's caution balanced each other out. "Mike always wanted to make sure he paid his own way," David Armstrong laughs. "Billie could give a shit. He was the baby. But Mike understood early. He made sure he graduated too. One night I was picking him up from guitar practice in my mom's station wagon. He was saying, 'I don't know about this.' It wasn't a big band breakup talk. The thing with Mike is that he's a worrier. And I think he was looking at it like 'Man, it's tough being a musician.' He wanted a fall-back. Mike grew up faster than Billie, and he wanted to make sure he wasn't left out in the cold. But he stuck with it."[12]

Armstrong wasn't going to be happy doing anything else, and so he forged ahead. He didn't have college classes or kids of his own to worry about: all he really had was a guitar, a bag of clothes, and a four-track recorder. He thrived on the chaos of punk rock living, and took it to its natural conclusion by moving into an abandoned warehouse in West Oakland with a tribe of other punk squatters. A network of these illegal crash pads was scattered around the East Bay; the refusal to shell out cash for the basic human need of shelter was (and still is) seen by some as a political statement. But the dangerous neighborhoods, filthy conditions, and broken windows made the overall experience far from ideal for Armstrong—much less his girlfriend. As Arica Paleno remembers, "I would stay with him sometimes in these warehouses full of crusty punks."[13]

Some of the crustiness rubbed off, to put it crudely—all that freedom can be a little much. "When we met them, Mike and Billie were seventeen," said Ben Weasel, of Lookout! labelmates Screeching Weasel. "We were staying up in the mountains at Lawrence Livermore's house, and we were so disgusted by these guys. We thought they were the biggest idiots we had ever met. They were so drunk that they were puking, and they were constantly smoking pot. So the next time I saw them, I was pretty wary but they came up and were really nice and clear-headed."[14]

One of their warehouse squats, above a West Oakland brothel, inspired the song "Welcome to Paradise," which appears on both *Kerplunk!* and *Dookie.* Armstrong had always had the ability to turn a bad situation into a good song, and he put it to good use in that song's description of how it feels to strike out on your own. "I've been fortunate to be part of the punk rock scene 'cause I see friends in Pinole and they're stuck in a rut," he said later. "An alternative lifestyle is a lot more fulfilling sometimes, just because you don't have money."[15] Over in San Francisco, Tré Cool of the Lookouts was discovering the same thing. "I lived a three-and-a-half hour drive away from San Francisco, so I'd come down to the city and stay for a week. We'd do a few shows, crash on the front couch, eat government cheese," he says. "My life was really about living dollar to dollar."[16]

Green Day was living show to show, but luckily the shows kept coming. They played a few bigger shows, including one with the Lookouts in Garberville in June of 1989: 1,300 people packed into the California Veterans' Hall.[17] Many venues, however, were just someone's basement, and the cops often shut them down because of noise complaints—but Green Day always had an acoustic guitar handy to keep the show going.

That same year, Armstrong and Dirnt began a longstanding tradition of playing in other bands occasionally. Armstrong briefly played guitar in the hardcore band Corrupted Morals, another Lookout! band; Dirnt sang for the Crummy Musicians (and probably lived up to the name). They got enough cash from helping out with other bands to help subsidize Green Day—their own band was always the number one concern.

THE RECORDS KEEP COMING

To keep the momentum going from their first EP, Lawrence Livermore sent the band back to the studio for a full-length album. On December 29, 1989, after Christmas when studio time was cheap, the band went into Art of Ears Studio in San Francisco and started recording at 4:30 p.m. Armstrong and Dirnt recorded their vocal parts at the same time, a money-saving measure that no major-label band would resort to. Twenty-four hours later, they had finished most of the recording. They went back and added guitar parts and harmonies, mixed the record, and by January 2, *39/Smooth* was done. It had cost $675 to make the ten-song album: about the same amount that Nirvana had spent to record their debut, *Bleach*, just a few months earlier.

Teenage heartache still provided inspiration, on songs like "At the Library" and "The Judge's Daughter," but darker, more reflective songs like "I Was There" hinted at the introspective hits that would come later such as "Good Riddance (Time of Your Life)" and "Wake Me Up When September Ends." In their melodic harmonies, Green Day drifted away from throat-shredding hardcore and closer to the Kinks, or even the Beatles.

The inspiration for the album title was a little more random. While they were holed up putting the last touches on the album, the band members had been using the word "smooth" a lot; it became sort of an inside joke, and they knew it had to be part of the title. At the same time, Armstrong's oldest brother Alan was turning thirty-nine, and jokingly told Armstrong that his band should mark the occasion on the album cover somehow. There you have it: *39/Smooth*.[18] Jesse Michaels, the former lead singer of Operation Ivy, contributed the cover design for the album: a black and white photograph of a girl in a cemetery. It's a little more somber than one would expect from a Green Day album, but at least the interior art was handled by Aaron Cometbus, who had a recognizably cartoonish touch.

39/Smooth didn't come out right away: to test the waters, the band went back to Art of Ears Studio in April of 1990 and banged out four more songs in a few hours for another seven-inch vinyl single. *Slappy* hit the streets in a rainbow of colors, including green (naturally), with Aaron Cometbus's art and layout. A cover of the Operation Ivy song "Knowledge" rounded off the EP; it's now one of the few early songs that Green Day continues to play live, sometimes with audience members sitting in on one instrument or another.

With two EPs on the streets and a full-length in the can, Armstrong was ready to go all in on the chance that his band could make it. On the day before his eighteenth birthday, February 16, 1990, he told his mother that he wouldn't be finishing high school. A high school dropout herself, she didn't force him to stay and finish the last few months. "When I was going in to drop out of high school," Armstrong laughs, "I gave one teacher my dropout slip. He just looked at me and said, 'Who are you?'"[19]

Cool also left high school, despite an outgoing personality that won him the position of class president. He passed the GED in his sophomore year and started studying music at a local junior college, working half the day and taking classes half the day. He played in the big band and the orchestra with local adults for about three semesters, learning to read music on the spot and use different kinds of percussion within one piece. "It was really cool," he remembers, "because most of the musicians were all these stuffy older dudes, and they were all really good players. But they had to let me play because I was like the only student there."[20]

Dirnt stayed in school, looking for the stability he didn't have as a kid, but he and Kiffmeyer continued to put most of their energy into the band. "The only thing I really wanted to do was live up to our potential, and that was it," says Armstrong, "We suddenly had this band that musically became pretty powerful, and we made a big noise. We just wanted to see where it could take us."[21] Armstrong told friends he'd become a pool cleaner or a TV repairman if the band didn't work out, but he didn't really doubt that it would. Nonetheless, when you aren't good at school, be it hard skills like homework or soft skills like hanging out with the cool kids, it's easy to get the message that you're a loser. That's a big part of what went into Green Day's early songs about pot smoking, heartache, and sitting around on the couch. "I was brainwashed to think that I was nothing compared to these people, these so-called geniuses who were teaching me all that crap," Armstrong said, "So I was like 'Okay, I'll be my own art form: being a f***** idiot, being a loser.' If that's what I was trained to think I am, then that's what I'm going to do, and I'm going to do it the best way I can. Now I'm 'losing' in a big way. But I still have nightmares about being behind in class."[22] The years of teenage loserdom paid off for Green Day, forcing the band members to find their own ways of expressing themselves and focusing on their strengths.

When Lookout! did finally release *39/Smooth*, the label trusted in the quality of the songs to spread the word; it didn't exactly have a lot of marketing muscle to put behind the album. Before the Internet and mp3s made it easy to share music and promote new bands, news about punk rock releases was limited to active zines like *Maximumrocknroll* in the Bay Area, *Flipside* in Los Angeles, and many other scattered outposts. Word of mouth was key, which helped level the playing field for many bands; no one could expect to sell thousands upon thousands of records or have gushing reviews plastered everywhere, so the bands who played the best shows and put out the best albums usually made their way to the top of the budding punk rock scene. This of course stands in stark contrast to the way things are more than twenty years later, when it often seems that whoever has the most marketing dollars behind them wins out.

The punk rock underground served Green Day well; Lookout! was able to spread the word beyond the Bay Area, and the album caught on. "Some of the bands that were coming through my studio were rocking it on a cassette and saying 'Check this out, man. Have you heard Green Day? They're really good!'" recalls Brett Gurewitz of LA's Bad Religion. "You know I liked how it was a little more pop, and it had like a sixties vibe."[23] Also in 1990, the Green Day song "I Want to Be Alone" appeared on the Flipside Records compilation *The Big One*. Compilations like this gave bands another way to get noticed outside their hometown—which was clearly this compilation's goal, as it featured Los Angeles bands including the Offspring on Side A, and San Francisco bands (many from the Gilman scene) on the other.

The next year, after the relative success of *39/Smooth*, Lookout! crammed all three of Green Day's earliest albums onto one record: *1,039 Smoothed Out Slappy Hours*. This album contained "I Want to Be Alone" as a bonus track, and is still in print today: it took until 2006, but it has officially gone gold in the U.S.

Green Day was a long way from going gold in 1990, but they threw themselves into working for the band, booking shows wherever they could. That included returning to Pinole Valley High School the same spring that Armstrong dropped out for a show with local band Separate Ways. Armstrong and future Green Day member Tré Cool got jobs selling newspaper subscriptions outside a supermarket near UC Berkeley. It only took a few hours before they cut out to spend the rest of the day smoking weed—and two days before they got fired.

WE'RE GONNA GET OUT OF THIS PLACE

Luckily, once again the band provided Armstrong with an escape. The next logical step for any band with a full-length album and a local following is to get out of town, and so, with help from the experienced Kiffmeyer, Green Day booked 45 shows around the country in the summer of 1990. Armstrong bought an orange Ford Econoline 150 van from his oldest brother Alan, and the band built lofts in the back for sleeping and storing equipment. Sean Hughes, the former bass player, joined in as roadie, and Kiffmeyer drove. They left the day Dirnt graduated from high school. "Billie and John were waiting for him on the street," remembers David Armstrong.[24] He jumped in the van and they took off.

"The tour was awesome," Hughes recalls. "We all got out of Rodeo, which we had all talked about: 'Man, I wanna do something. I wanna go somewhere besides here.' We'd hung out in Berkeley, but we'd never seen the country. We were totally on our own."[25] They had scraped together some money for the trip, but not much: most of what they lived on came from the little they got paid after each show. They also made money by selling albums and DIY merchandise, printing T-shirts on top of their guitar cases. "People would bring along their own shirts and we'd just charge them for the print," says Dirnt. "That's what kept us on the road and sold us a lot of independent albums."[26] With Aaron Cometbus on board as roadie and occasional substitute drummer, punk survival was assured: his zine, later collected in the book *Despite Everything*, covers eating out of dumpsters, traveling the United States, punk collectives, and musings on anarchy, in a clear embodiment of punk rock life. Green Day played a huge variety of shows, with anywhere from 5 to 500 people in the audience. One bootleg video from this tour, at the Paint Factory in Tampa, Florida, reveals that Green Day sounded just as poppy and jangly back then as they do now, weakening any argument that the band softened their sound later to sell more records.[27]

They weren't even old enough to drink yet, so most shows were on college campuses. At one of these shows in Minneapolis, the eighteen-year-old Armstrong met twenty-two-year-old Adrienne Nesser, a dark-haired, dreadlocked sociology student. Even though he had just dropped out of high school, he was excited, not intimidated, when he talked to her. "Billie Joe and I met on the very first Green Day tour when Al Sobrante was in the band. I was one of only ten people at a Green Day gig and me and Billie ended up hitting it off," she recalls.[28] She was living in a small town called Mankato and attending Minnesota State—and she had a boyfriend, coincidentally named Billy. Armstrong was still dating Arica Paleno at that point, and so the two did nothing but talk. Luckily, Minneapolis had a strong indie scene, and so Green Day was able to land more than one show and hang around town longer than usual for a touring band.

While they were there, the band recorded four songs for an EP on the cheap: "Sweet Children," "Best Thing in Town," "Strangeland," and a cover of The Who's "My Generation." The album is confusingly titled *Sweet Children*, and the sound quality is very "punk rock." "It was done cheap and fast and sounds crappy," says Larry Livermore, "and therefore many people think it is the oldest Green Day record, but it isn't."[29] Jeff Spiegel released the EP in late 1990 on his label Skene! Records. The first pressing was only 1,500 copies on pink and black vinyl, and the second pressing, just 600 copies, was plain black vinyl. Rumors of a third pressing abound, but the first two pressings are already very rare and prized by collectors, although the songs were added to the re-release of *Kerplunk!* Skene! went on to put out albums by other great punk bands, such as Jawbreaker and the Hard-Ons, in the 1990s.

When Green Day left Minneapolis, Armstrong and Nesser exchanged phone numbers, and he called her from the road whenever he felt like he needed to talk to someone. "I remember on the way back, he was trying to take a picture of a road sign that said 80," remembers Sean Hughes, "because he was thinking of Adrienne and he called her 'Aidy.'"[30]

Armstrong and Paleno broke up soon after the tour ended. The two stayed friends, but he never stopped thinking about Nesser. He barely knew her, but she had already gotten under his skin and become a muse for him. She first inspired the song "2,000 Light Years Away," and, later in his career, inspired indirect love songs like "80," a take-off on his nickname for her, and direct songs like "Church on Sunday," about working through a fight.

In July, Armstrong chipped in some lead guitar parts and backup vocals for the Lookouts' four-track single, *IV*. The band broke up soon after that, though—all the members were living in different towns at that point—and the record was released posthumously.

THE BEAT OF A DIFFERENT DRUMMER

At around the same time, unbeknownst to Dirnt and Armstrong, Kiffmeyer was making plans to go off to Humboldt State College in Arcata, California, that fall—almost 300 miles away. Armstrong only found out by accident. "Me and Aaron Elliot were walking around in Benicia with a couple of girls," Armstrong recalls, "and Stacy was like, 'Yeah, everybody's leaving town this summer, going away to college, etc.,' and then she mentioned that John was going away to college, too. And I'm like, 'John's leaving? What do you mean, John's leaving?' And Aaron looked at me and goes, 'Oh man, he didn't tell you, did he?'"[31] Armstrong didn't even know if he wanted the band to continue without Kiffmeyer. He certainly didn't want to wait around and play only on the drummer's breaks from school. But at the same time, the band was all he and Dirnt had going: neither of them had any plans to go back to school, and it's not like they had satisfying careers on the side.

Armstrong, ever the overachiever, decided to put the band first and move on without Kiffmeyer. "John had options," says Armstrong. "He had opportunities, like being able to go to school. And I don't have anything against that, but I didn't want to feel like anybody's side project. And that's the way I was starting to feel with John."[32] They got Dave EC, drummer for Filth and the Wynona Ryders, to play drums for a few weeks, but he left without ever recording for the band (although he got a credit on *Kerplunk!*).

Armstrong and Dirnt already knew Tré Cool from Gilman and playing with the Lookouts, although Armstrong's session with the Lookouts in July was the first time they had played together. They asked him to jam, he agreed, and they played their first show together in November 1990. They took it cautiously at first; as Paleno says, "Tré kind of had a bad reputation for being a real prankster and a real jokester. And I remember Billie telling me, 'Well, he's a great drummer and we like him, but he's just one of those people you gotta keep an eye on because you never know what he's gonna say. Whether it's going to get you kicked out of a club or off a show.' But when Tré joined the band, *bam*—they just took off. They were that much better. He was the missing element. Plus John wasn't a pot smoker and Tré was, and that really was the Green Day common thread, the pot smoking."[33]

His prankster reputation ended up working for the band rather than against it. "I think the biggest element Tré added in addition to being one of the best drummers in rock 'n' roll was the whole zany, crazy thing," says Chris Appelgren of Lookout! Records. "Billie and Mike always came across as a little more serious and quiet before Tré joined the band."[34] Dirnt and Armstrong embraced the wild side of their drummer, who brought out a little of their own craziness.

But Kiffmeyer wasn't done with the band yet—the weird, drawn-out breakup lasted through a big show at the Phoenix Theater in Petaluma, north of San Francisco, when Green Day was scheduled to open for punk pioneers Bad Religion. Kiffmeyer and Cool both came expecting to play, and the mini-showdown ended with Kiffmeyer playing the show. "And I was like, wait a minute," Armstrong remembers, "Tré has been working with us for months, and you come down to play this one gig. That doesn't seem fair to Tré, who by then was becoming a good friend of ours."[35]

"I think that experience of [Kiffmeyer] wanting the band to exist at his convenience and on his terms made them realize they couldn't do that," says Appelgren. "They weren't at college, and they wanted to keep moving on. I think John thought, 'Well, this is my band. I'm gonna come down and play the show.' He played the show, but I think it was his last one because of how he did that. I think they felt bullied by it."[36]

It was hard for Armstrong to stand up to the older musician; after all, he'd brought a lot to Green Day and was far more experienced. But he came forward as the band's true leader, and Green Day moved on. Kiffmeyer did help out with the production on *Kerplunk!*, and he stayed active in punk rock with the bands the Ne'er Do Wells and the Lookout!-signed band the High Fives, but he didn't play with the band after that last show. They went far beyond what he had imagined. "They were really going to take the spirit of the underdog and the misfit to a larger level in their own way," Appelgren says. "I think that to me is tremendous and something to be proud of and maybe John didn't have the vision to do that."[37]

One of the first new places they took punk rock was to a broader teen audience. With the older Kiffmeyer, this clearly wasn't going to happen, but now that Cool was on board, they all *were* teenagers, and they became unlikely local heartthrobs. Regular high school girls started coming to Green Day shows in the East Bay to sing along to Armstrong's love songs. Punks in the scene looked down on them, making fun of the typical suburban girl "Trout Dance": standing with their arms folded, shaking their ponytails so they looked like a trout on a hook. "They were huge in Petaluma," laughs Sean Hughes. "And there were all these hot chicks that were into them over there."[38] If Green Day could get Petaluma high school girls to listen to punk rock, they could get anyone to listen—or at least enough people to justify taking their new lineup cross-country.

NOTES

1. Marc Spitz, *Nobody Likes You: Inside the Turbulent Life, Times, and Music of Green Day* (New York: Hyperion, 2006), 64.
2. Ben Myers, *Green Day: American Idiots and the New Punk Explosion* (New York: The Disinformation Company, Inc. 2006), 53.
3. Myers, 51.
4. Myers, 51.
5. Spitz, 65.
6. Myers, 50.
7. John Colapinto, "Working Class Heroes." *Rolling Stone*, November 17, 2005, 52.
8. Ibid., 52.
9. Ibid., 52.
10. Spitz, 62.
11. Ibid., 47.
12. Ibid., 47.
13. Spitz, 48.
14. Myers, 55.
15. Ibid., 55.
16. Ibid., 49.
17. Doug Small, *Omnibus Press Presents the Story of: Green Day* (New York: Omnibus Press, 2005), 15.
18. Myers, 60.
19. Chris Mundy, "Green Daze." *Rolling Stone*, January 26, 1995, 38.
20. Matt Peiken, "Green Day's Tré Cool: Hungry for Drumming," *Modern Drummer*, May 1998, 50.
21. Spitz, 46-47.
22. Myers, 57.
23. Spitz, 66-67.
24. Ibid., 67.
25. Ibid., 67.
26. Myers, 65.
27. Ibid., 64.
28. Adrienne Nesser, quoted in "FAQ," www.greenday.net/faq.html (accessed December 10, 2008).
29. Myers, 66.
30. Spitz, 68.
31. Lawrence Livermore, "Lawrence Livermore Interview," http://greenday.net/livermore.htm (accessed December 10, 2008).
32. Ibid.
33. Spitz, 71.
34. Ibid., 72.

35. Lawrence Livermore, http://greenday.net/livermore.htm (accessed December 10, 2008).

36. Spitz, 73.

37. Ibid., 74.

38. Ibid., 75.

CHAPTER THREE

Local Heroes

In 1991, with their lineup and their base of hometown fans solidified, Green Day lined up the first tour with Tré Cool on drums and brought a couple of friends along to help sell merchandise and load gear. Once again, they played a scattered assortment of punk houses, community centers, skate parks, and dive bars across the U.S., depending on the kindness of fans to show up and pull together enough money to get them to the next town. During one show in New Orleans, someone broke into the van and stole all their bags and the cash they'd earned so far. With no money for gas and no extra clothes, the Green Day crew drove through the night to their next stop, the college town of Auburn, Alabama. They played in a living room for a few dozen punks and students, who donated clothes and money to keep the tour going. Meeting such generous people at such a low point was a humbling experience for the band. They earned enough that night to get them to Birmingham, Alabama, where they earned enough to get to the next show, and so on.

The rock 'n' roll routine of driving for hours every day, sleeping anywhere they could, and eating whatever was cheap—all for the sake of that one amazing hour on stage—turned the band into a tight-knit unit. The never-ending string of shows allowed Cool to mesh with Billie Joe Armstrong and Mike Dirnt and move from learning John

Kiffmeyer's drum parts to developing his own style. Cool describes finally clicking with Dirnt's bass, saying, "My foot just locked in with his right hand. We never worked on it in a conscious sense. It just came from playing together so much that we finally knew what each other was going to do."[1]

Within a small but growing circle of punks, Green Day had made a name for itself. During this first tour with Tré, the established indie label IRS Records allegedly approached the band. Founder Miles Copeland, brother of the Police's drummer Stewart Copeland, had signed punk and new wave bands like the Damned, the Go-Go's, and the Buzzcocks, and had also gotten behind R.E.M. early on. But even though it sounded like a solid opportunity, Green Day knew they weren't ready. At the Birmingham show, Dirnt talked to some of the fans and explained that signing with IRS would mean tour buses and hotels, cutting off the direct connection with their audience that they had just started to build. They continued on across the country in their van, honing their approach on older songs and developing new ones.

RECORDING *KERPLUNK!*

In May, they went back to Art of Ears Studio with Andy Ernst producing. The low-level success of *39/Smooth* meant that they could spend double the money recording the follow-up: all of $2,000. They did two short sessions in May and two in September to re-record some of the material, staying true to their roots by keeping it quick and cheap. Armstrong and Dirnt even recorded lead and backup vocals at the same time to cut costs. The list of thank-yous in the liner notes included Adrienne Nesser, whom Armstrong still called to talk through things in his life.

Former drummer Kiffmeyer is credited (under his alias Al Sobrante) as executive producer. This marked the last of Kiffmeyer's involvement with the band, as he settled into life at Humboldt State University, started a bike-repair business, and began playing regularly with Lookout! band the Ne'er Do Wells. His relationship with Armstrong and Dirnt suffered, as Armstrong let on in occasional interviews near that time, but has since improved, and the band members speak well of him now.

The last album he helped create showed Green Day's new sense of confidence. They still alternate between scatological jokes and love songs, but the music pulls the two sides together into a more solid style. The weird S&M country of Cool's "Dominated Love Slave" sits comfortably alongside introspective songs like "2,000 Light Years Away" and "Christie Road," inspired by Nesser and Arica Paleno, respectively.

They had a little free time after recording was finished, and Armstrong was able to squeeze in a little quality time with his side project Pinhead Gunpowder. Aaron Cometbus (formerly the drummer for Crimpshrine) had originally formed the band as a loose association of punks in Arcata, California—Green Day had dropped him off on one of their tours, and he'd stayed. He moved back to Berkeley around 1991, and, in order to keep playing the songs, formed another loose group of friends who all had other bands. Armstrong joined on guitar, along with Mike Kersh of Fuel. Bill Schneider of Monsula played bass. In 1994, future Green Day touring guitarist Jason White joined. Everyone knew that Pinhead Gunpowder would have to be a part-time project, but the garage-band situation suited everyone just fine. They released their first song, "Benecia by the Bay," on the Lookout! compilation *Can of Pork* in January 1992, alongside East Bay bands like the Lookouts and Fifteen, and have since released more than ten EPs and albums. Ironically, they've managed to outlast almost all of the other bands its members have belonged to—except Green Day, of course.

TRANSATLANTIC PUNK

By the time *Kerplunk* went off to the record pressing plant, Green Day was getting ready for their first tour overseas. It's another reminder of the band's staying power to think that back then smoking was still allowed on flights. "How many bands can claim they toured Europe back when you could still smoke on the plane?" Dirnt laughed in 2005.[2] And they were barely old enough to smoke—all of them were just nineteen.

The band spent three months in Europe, two of those in Germany, with most of the sixty-four shows booked at low-rent, unconventional venues through a well-connected American friend living in the UK. The tour was almost completely self-funded: the band saved their meager royalty checks and touring income to pay for their plane tickets and van rental. They earned money for day-to-day expenses (such as food) along the way. Green Day albums were only available by mail-order in Europe, so the band smuggled albums to sell in their luggage.

They also brought the photo negative for their T-shirt design and had a screen made in Germany so they could silk-screen shirts as needed, just like they'd done on their first tour. After the first week, when they discovered that it's a Danish tradition for punks to throw beer at bands they like, their instruments were toast. (Luckily—for him—Armstrong had brought Lawrence Livermore's amp instead of his own.) Replacing the instruments was out of the question, as they were barely earning enough money to keep everyone fed and traveling from show to show. The band ended up borrowing new equipment every night. "Seriously," says Cool, "I was using guys' kits where the drummer would say, 'If you screw up my kit, I'm gonna stab you.'"[3]

The German squats where Green Day spent most of their time could get a little scary: because their illegal warehouse encampments were subject to raids by police or their neo-Nazi adversaries, many had stashes of ski masks, buckets of rocks, and slings, ready for battle. One night, a friend who was traveling with the band jokingly asked a woman working the door what she'd do if he snatched the money; she calmly pulled out a .45 handgun and told him she'd shoot him.[4]

Things calmed down a little in the UK, although the band was intimidated at first to be playing in the country that spawned the Beatles and Led Zeppelin. The British punks were friendly, and they played more pub shows, which, though far from glamorous, offered a step up from only playing squats. For most of the tour, though, their more danceable sound didn't exactly fit in on the typical bill. As Armstrong told *NME* in 2005, "There were five bands on the bill, four of which sounded like Napalm Death. Then there was us."[5]

Living by their wits and talent, improvising with new equipment every night, the band members grew even closer as the tour stretched on. Just reaching out to a foreign audience took a special kind of charisma. "It made us a really good band, playing on different equipment and in different situations," Armstrong said later. "I think it made us better because obviously there's a language difference and it meant we had to be more animated and project a bit more physically."[6]

On December 17, 1991, Green Day got the first finished copies of *Kerplunk!* At the moment, the bandmates were in Southampton, in southern England, getting ready for a show with Jailcell. They decided to make the show an impromptu record release party, despite being more than five thousand miles away from the East Bay. Green Day treated their audience to a set list full of future hits from *Kerplunk!*, including "Welcome to Paradise," "2,000 Light Years Away," and "Christie Road." The band members threw on all the weird

European clothes they had been collecting, and Armstrong fell off the stage—a show to remember.

Possibly even more memorable, the Christmas Eve show in Wigan (near Beatles hometown Liverpool) involved a truly raunchy theatrical production. All the bands on the bill decided to do something special to celebrate the holiday: one band dressed as the Sex Pistols, another dressed as KISS, and Green Day decided to re-enact the Nativity scene. Dirnt played Santa Claus, Cool played the Virgin Mary, and Armstrong was the schizophrenic three wise men. Their friend Aidan played a midwife, and their long-haired friend Sean was Jesus. "Tré was up on a table with his legs spread out giving birth to Sean, who was under the table with a plastic carrier bag that was full of a bunch of ketchup, tomato soup, and rice pudding, which we then threw on the audience," Dirnt remembers fondly. "Some of it landed on this poor guy wearing glasses. Some people were eating it. We thought it was f***** funny."[7]

"It was a bad idea that just got worse," Armstrong laughs. "It was kind of the finale of the night—silly string and beer everywhere. I don't think we fully recovered from that, because by the time we actually played people had seen it all."[8]

The band returned home in February 1992 with a stash of memories (sleeping next to a head in a jar of formaldehyde), a new understanding of foreign cultures (there are no distortion pedals in Poland), and some new friends (i.e., Armstrong's case of head lice).

A RENAISSANCE BEGINS

While Green Day was gallivanting around Europe, *Kerplunk!* was released in the United States on January 17. The landscape of pop music had changed dramatically between the time they finished recording and the time the album hit stores. On September 24, 1991, Sub Pop Records had released Nirvana's second album, *Nevermind.* The same month that *Kerplunk* came out, *Nevermind* booted Michael Jackson out of the number one slot on the Billboard charts. Major labels began scouting for new rock bands, and radio started giving smaller bands the time of day. Suddenly, melodic punk rock seemed a lot more marketable.

Even if Green Day had hit a sophomore slump with *Kerplunk!,* they could have spun it into more success, thanks to the new, punk-friendly environment. But *Kerplunk!* was truly another leap forward, and punk fanzines like *Flipside* and *Maximumrocknroll* caught on, as did farsighted national magazines like *College Music Journal* (*CMJ*). "The twelve chunks of fun on *Kerplunk!* favor melody over speed metal aggression and lyrics of love and confusion over explosive revolutionary tracks," the *CMJ* editors wrote in the January 31, 1991 issue. "The hooks in these songs are as easy to find as a broken string must be at a Green Day show. Keenly underscored by gleeful, chiming vocals and hurdle-jumping bassines, Green Day's tunes stick in your head like cat hair."[9]

The dour, heavy grunge sound of Seattle had a much different style and approach than the often-goofy Gilman aesthetic—not to mention that Green Day members had short hair. Still, Green Day caught the wave that washed out overproduced pop like Paula Abdul and Bryan Adams in the early 1990s. According to Lawrence Livermore, *Kerplunk!* sold ten thousand copies the first day, an unheard of amount for an independent punk record. By comparison, Operation Ivy's album *Energy*, Lookout!'s previous all-time bestseller, took a year to sell two thousand copies. By the end of 1992, *Kerplunk!* would sell another twenty thousand copies.

When the band got back from Europe, the label was reeling from the overwhelming fan response to *Kerplunk!* Roadies at the band's first stateside shows reported hundreds of people attending in towns where the band used to draw fifty. The world had changed.

College radio caught on, amplifying the local phenomenon and spreading it across the country, as they had started doing a few years before with R.E.M. "People just grabbed a hold of them," says Matt Pinfield, at the time a college radio DJ at Rutgers in New Jersey. "Eighteen- through twenty-one-year-old kids who were sneaking into bars were into Green Day. They knew *Kerplunk!* They knew *39/Smooth*. And they were spreading the word among their friends. . . . I think the thing that made people grab hold of it was that it had such a pop element to it. They represented a complete turn in punk from the hard-core to the pop-informed."[10]

THE BOOKMOBILE TOUR

Punk was no longer restricted to a tiny clubhouse of outcasts— Green Day's accessible yet aggressive tunes spread the word to more and more people across the country. Because none of them had a permanent address (Armstrong still had his stuff stored at his mother's house), they eagerly hit the road again.

This time, they traveled in style. Tré Cool's father, Frank Wright II, who owned a small trucking business, overhauled a used bookmobile for the band by ripping out the bookshelves and building lofts for storage and sleeping. He also served as their driver on three tours, although he sometimes couldn't help but slip back into dad mode. "It was fine until he started crossing the line of—of like, being a father and being a bus driver. Like he would complain about dirty socks and stuff," Cool recalled later. "It's like, 'Dude, we're a punk band. We *are* dirty socks.'"[11]

Aside from their laundry problem, Cool's father came to respect his son and his friends over the course of the tour. "I watched them go from a bunch of kids to a group of musicians with a work ethic," he told *Rolling Stone*. "On their first tour or two, it was more of a party than anything else. I still scratch my head and say, 'How in the hell did they make it?'"[12] Through sheer hard work, Green Day was creating momentum for itself. The band started filling well-known clubs like the Whisky A Go Go in LA and Slim's in San Francisco, mostly through word of mouth. More people sang along as *Kerplunk!* slowly spread beyond the East Bay.

Of course, everybody needs a break, and the bookmobile made a good hideaway—except when people didn't recognize its new function. "We had one lady walk into the bookmobile," Dirnt told *Stuff* magazine in 2004. "We were smoking so much weed. Back then, we just smoked pot all the time. It was pretty funny. She walks in, and she's standing there for a second. She looks and goes, 'Oh! This isn't a bookmobile, is it?' She got all the way into the vehicle in a cloud of smoke."[13]

The band went back to Europe in 1992, and continued touring the United States when they got back, lining up show after show. "I remember working the LA clubs, and these bratty kids showed up," Warped Tour founder Kevin Lyman, then a booker, told MTV. "They had such attitude, but as soon as they played, it was like, 'Anything I can do to help you guys.'"[14] The band's popularity grew gradually but measurably; Cool remembers how fast they started going through merchandise: "We'd take the forty bucks that we'd managed to not spend on gas," he said, "go to a K-Mart and buy up all the large and extra-large white cotton T-shirts, then go to the house of someone who had a hose and enough space to hang out a bunch of shirts.

Then we'd screen-print them on Billie's guitar case—two dozen shirts—and sell them at the next gig. We got to where we were buying out the K-Marts. You know you're doing well when you're able to buy all the T-shirts at a K-Mart!"[15]

Everyone involved with the band took pride in their successes, seeing a victory for the DIY ethic of punk rock. "And we [at the label]," recalls Chris Appelgren, then a Lookout! employee, "with each milestone we achieved, thought: 'Well, gee, we can thumb our nose at the rest of the world for being such idiots before.'"[16]

GROWING PAINS

As Green Day's visibility grew, the mechanics of being a band got more and more complicated. Small shows would get canceled, and they'd end up playing nasty mid-sized clubs and bars. Fast-talking promoters ripped off the band; clueless roughnecks showed up at small venues and started fights. The band had to cancel more than one show when far too many fans tried to get in. Something had to give: the band clearly couldn't keep doing things the same old way.

Thus, Green Day signed with their first managers, lawyers Elliott Cahn and Jeff Saltzman of Cahnman Management. The company had rounded up several modern rock bands after the success of *Nevermind*, and had previously managed the Melvins, Mudhoney, and Primus. They later went on to manage the Offspring, Pennywise, Rancid, and other punk bands.

At the time, Green Day had a reputation for not wanting anything to do with anyone in the music business. "I think more than being antagonistic, they were cautious and worried," says Cahn. "I don't think they wanted a bunch of cigar chewers."[17] Cahn and Saltzman must not have seemed like cigar-smoking suits, because they went on to manage Green Day for years. Right from the start, they started promoting Green Day in a whole new way, sending demos to major labels and bringing the labels' A&R (artists and repertoire) representatives to shows across the country.

At the same time that the band started weighing the possibility of moving to a major label, Lookout! came to realize that they couldn't do everything for Green Day that Green Day wanted to do. "We don't have the ability to get them on MTV, or to be on all commercial radio stations or into every record store in the land," Livermore said in 1994. "Depending on your beliefs, that might be an advantage or a drawback. But undoubtedly a large factor in Green Day choosing the path they did was the fact that they wanted to do these things."[18]

There's some subtle punk rock criticism in Livermore's words, which was echoed at the time by many people who knew the band— even Armstrong's girlfriend at the time, a fiercely punk rock Berkeley student named Amanda. She published her own zine, went to shows at Gilman, and resolutely tried to live outside the boundaries of corporate America. Naturally, she was attracted to Armstrong, but she was repelled by the thought of art being exploited for profit by a major label. Some friends thought that a major label deal presented too many risks: if the band became a one-hit wonder or their album tanked, their careers would be over and they'd have nothing to fall back on. After all, Armstrong never even finished high school. It seemed safer to continue building their reputation within the punk rock community, where they had a solid base. It also seemed like classic sell-out behavior to abandon their grass-roots community for the sake of going national—but Green Day knew they had what it would take to reach a wide audience, and they had bigger dreams for their music than entertaining an exclusive crew of friends in their Gilman Street clubhouse. They wanted to test themselves on a bigger stage; they didn't want to play it safe. "We were already on Lookout!, which I thought was the ultimate independent label, so we didn't really want to go to a bigger independent label," Armstrong recalled later. "If we were going to make the switch, let's take a real chance."[19]

MAKING THE LEAP

They knew how their fellow punk rockers would react to talk of them moving to a major label, but they managed to keep it light. Mark Hoppus of Blink-182, one of the first bands to ride the Green Day wave to success, remembers seeing the band in 1992 or early 1993 in San Diego: "I remember it was funny because all the talk was that Green Day were gonna be signed to a major label, and back then there were lots of arguments as to whether people should sign to major labels. Billie Joe was onstage and he said, 'Hey everyone, make sure you clap really loud because the executives from the label are trying to decide whether they want to sign us or not tonight, so let them know what you think.' He was making a joke out of it which was pretty cool."[20]

They turned the bidding war into a joke on the record companies for a while, as well, treating eager A&R representatives like meal tickets. The labels understood the numbers, even if they didn't always understand the music: Green Day had sold 60,000 records, without any real promotion or distribution, while touring two continents on their own. Clearly, they had talent, the ambition, and the work ethic to make the most of it. A stream of A&R men (still mostly men at the time) came by their basement apartment on Ashby Street in Berkeley, and while their wives went shopping on Telegraph Avenue, they watched the band practice and tried to get them to sign on. "Warner Bros., Geffen, Sony, and everybody's mother wanted to sign us, but we held off for quite a long time," said Cool. "Why? Because David Geffen's money was paying for us to go to Disneyland. We kind of milked them. We wanted to hold out until we got complete artistic control. . . . We thought, 'F*** this, it's our lives.' It's like getting married or something."[21] Armstrong, Dirnt, and Cool put some serious thought into what label they would choose and how they would go about signing on. They had seen many punk bands in the '80s sign to major labels and compromise their sound; that path was not for them. What they wanted was just the opportunity to create a bigger version of their own sound.

Total creative control came first on Green Day's list of demands for any label that approached them. This didn't seem like an outrageous request; in the early '90s, the band members observed, record labels had become a little more hands-off than before. Warner Bros. in particular had a reputation as an artist-friendly label. For one thing, they had R.E.M., who had jumped over from the indie label IRS Records three years earlier. Reprise, the subsidiary that ultimately went after Green Day, was founded by Frank Sinatra; it had put out all of Jimi Hendrix's albums and some of the best albums by the Kinks and Neil Young. Another subsidiary, Sire Records, had an enviable lineup of American and British bands, from the punk of the Ramones to Echo and the Bunnymen's post-punk to the new wave of Talking Heads—not to mention Armstrong's beloved Replacements.

Despite its reputation, however, Warner Bros. was in a bit of a slump. For every R.E.M., they had dozens of flops. Rapper Ice-T's metal project, Body Count, drew a lot of bad publicity in the spring and summer of 1992 for the song "Cop Killer." Madonna wasn't doing so hot at the moment, either. The label needed something to keep the engines running.

Junior A&R man Rob Cavallo also badly needed a hit. He had recently produced the debut album from the Los Angeles band the

Muffs, which Green Day had heard and liked. It was a great pop-punk album, but it never took off for Warner Bros., and neither had many of Cavallo's other projects. Cavallo had enough drive and talent not to give up, though. He grew up in the music business—his father was Prince's manager during the *Purple Rain* era, and raised his son on a steady diet of Beatles records. Cavallo spent all his money on gear as a teenager, learning to play a range of instruments and teaching himself to produce. When he started looking for a music-industry job, he never rested on his father's reputation. He produced a demo for the long-forgotten band Rhythm Core and sent it to Warner Bros. in 1987; they didn't sign the band, but they brought Cavallo on staff. By 1993, he hadn't brought the label any real hits. "But you know what was great about Warner Bros. at that time and still is today?" Cavallo says. "They really allow you the chance—they saw something in me that I didn't even know was there."[22]

Green Day's demo ended up with Cavallo, and he went down to Berkeley to meet the band. He sat on a bucket in the same basement room where the "Longview" video was later filmed and watched the band play for about forty minutes. Then, having heard that he could play a bunch of Beatles songs, the band members got him stoned and got a jam session going. When Cavallo presented his argument for why Green Day should sign with him, the band members listened—but they also had something to say for themselves. As Cavallo remembers it, "They were like, 'We think we need the help of Reprise to realize our potential; however, we are fully confident that we are going to do it on our own anyway. So you're going to take the record that we make and you're going to send it to radio stations for us. So when they hear it, they're going to like it and they're going to want to play it.'"[23] Green Day impressed Cavallo with their confidence and talent, and Cavallo impressed them with his authentic appreciation of their music. Soon after, the August 24, 1993, edition of the *San Francisco Chronicle* announced a deal: "The buzz on the band is that Green Day, a not so oblique reference to pot smoking, is a grassroots phenomenon poised to break big with the release of a major-label debut early next year."[24]

Before plunging into the world of buzz and big breaks, Green Day played two last shows at 924 Gilman as an independent band. Their official final show took place on September 24, 1993, and bootleg recordings are still passed around. One last under-the-radar show with Brent's TV drew 150 friends through word of mouth, including Larry Livermore. "Almost everyone knew each other and knew the words to all the songs by both bands," he recalls. "So we were all dancing and signing along together, and it was warm and festive and family-like, but there was also this bitter-sweet feeling that came from knowing that things would never be like this again, that this was the last time we'd all be together this way."[25] Green Day knew they were in for a change, but they had no idea how fast it would come.

NOTES

1. Matt Peiken, "Green Day's Tré Cool: Hungry for Drumming," *Modern Drummer*, May 1998, 49.
2. Ben Myers, *Green Day: American Idiots and the New Punk Explosion* (New York: The Disinformation Company, Inc. 2006), 75.
3. Peiken, 49.
4. Myers, 78.
5. Doug Small, *Omnibus Press Presents the Story of: Green Day* (New York: Omnibus Press, 2005), 19.
6. Victoria Durham, "Green Day: Let the Good Times Roll," *Rock Sound*, March 2005, 51.
7. Myers, 80.
8. Ibid., 80.
9. Marc Spitz, *Nobody Likes You: Inside the Turbulent Life, Times, and Music of Green Day* (New York: Hyperion, 2006), 76.
10. Ibid., 77.
11. Tracy Smith, "Green Day Having the Time of Their Lives," CBS.com, May 24, 2009, http://www.cbsnews.com/stories/2009/05/24/sunday/main5037160.shtml (accessed May 31, 2009).
12. Chris Mundy, "Green Daze," *Rolling Stone*, January 26, 1995, 39.
13. Small, 19.
14. Joe D'Angelo, "How Green Day's *Dookie* Fertilized a Punk-Rock Revival," mtv.com (accessed December 9, 2008).
15. *Guitar World* editors, "Green Day: The Complete History," *Guitar World Presents Guitar Legends*, June 2005, 13.
16. Spitz, 79.
17. Small, 22.
18. Myers, 89.
19. *Guitar World* editors, 14.
20. Myers, 90.
21. Ibid., 92.
22. Spitz, 85.
23. Myers, 93.
24. Spitz, 81.
25. Small, 24.

CHAPTER FOUR

The Big Splash

"I think I might have been the first person [Tré] told that they got signed up as Green Day with the first major label," said Zann Cannon Goff, Tré Cool's old school friend. "I used to work at Whole Foods Market. And I was a cashier. Tré would come in regularly because he was living near there. So he comes in one day buying a bunch of cookies and chips and stuff and looking all glassy eyed, and he's like 'You'll never guess what just happened.' And I'm like, 'What?' He's like, 'This guy from Reprise Records just came over and he got us stoned and signed a record deal with us. We're gonna be really big.' And in the back of my mind I'm like, 'Yeah right, whatever.' Who the heck out of Willits is gonna be on MTV? Then it was three months later and there he is on MTV. That day was the last time I saw him. I was pretty damn shocked. Definitely jealous."[1] Many of Green Day's friends and acquaintances felt the same way as the word got out that they had signed to a major label. *Maximumrocknroll* ran anti-Green Day letters to the editor by the bucketful (yet still refuse to talk to biographers about the band). "Can you imagine what it feels like to pick up that magazine, something you totally respect, and read all these f****** opinions about you?" Armstrong said in *Spin*.[2]

IN THE STUDIO

The pressure of having almost everyone they knew waiting to see them fail sent the band members into the studio ready to prove themselves. Billie Joe Armstrong and Mike Dirnt had a years-long history of turning inward to focus on music in hard times, and Cool, by now, was an essential part of that. They put their focus on the music, really thinking through who they were and how to express that by making a statement, even an anti-statement. With *Kerplunk!*, they had moved so fast that the record didn't serve as a defining statement, but with *Dookie*, their first album on a major label, they were determined to show the world the real Green Day.

Cavallo was right there with them. "My mantra as a producer at that time was, I want you to sound like the best version of yourselves," he recalled later. "I think *Dookie* is a really good snapshot of what Green Day sounded like at that time. And that's why I think it works: because it's honest. That's not only why it works, but also why we didn't get killed. I didn't turn out to be the evil record producer who killed Green Day's sound."[3] The band didn't take well to being produced for the first time—in the past, they had only had engineers present, whose job was just to get a quality recording done and stay out of the way. A producer offers far more guidance. It's important to note that Green Day has a co-producer credit on *Dookie* and every album after that, however. They settled in at Fantasy Studios in Berkeley, where bands such as Creedence Clearwater Revival and Aerosmith had recorded (and where punk bands such as Rancid and Jawbreaker would eventually record), and spent five weeks recording more songs than they would ever need. Still, they kept their focus: Armstrong recorded all of his vocals in two days, many of them in single takes. Between sessions, they'd go to a Mexican restaurant down the street, where the still-underage Cool could always get a drink. And, let's be honest, the group probably had more than one "green day" in the studio.

The whole album is a testament to "youthful indiscretions" and adolescent angst, from the self-disgust on album opener "Burnout" to the hidden track "All By Myself," Cool's obnoxiously hilarious ode to stalking. The album opens with three chunks of loud, catchy punk rock (all of which come in under three minutes) before the deceptively laid-back bass intro to "Longview" breaks in. "I was playing a lot of jazz so really that was a shuffle," he explains.[4] The other ingredient, besides jazz and punk rock, was LSD. Dirnt famously wrote half of the tricky bass line on drugs. "I was laying up against the wall with my bass lying on my lap," Dirnt told *Rolling Stone*. "It just came to me. I said, 'Bill, check this out. Isn't that the wackiest thing you've ever heard?' Later, it took me a long time to be able to play it, but it made sense when I was on drugs."[5] They tried a few studio tricks to enhance the message of questioning your sanity, but didn't ultimately use them. "There was a version of it where we put this doctor speaking in the background," Cavallo recalls. "He's talking about all these various sexual dysfunctional diseases related to impotence and things. That's something that is brilliant and is on tape somewhere but didn't make it to the record."[6] It's probably for the best—although fans would drool over the alternate version now, the original has a simple raw power that doesn't need embellishment. They kept "Longview" true to its roots by bringing in their old friend Eggplant, the one who told them about Gilman in the first place. At shows, when they sang the line "Call me pathetic, call me what you will," Eggplant always shouted from the audience, "What you will!" So he came by the studio to record that part—it's just audible through headphones.

"Pulling Teeth" connects back to a pillow fight gone wrong: the always accident-prone Dirnt started it with his girlfriend Anastasia at a friend's house. He ran around a corner, pillow raised high, and ran into a beam, breaking both his elbows—but luckily, not his skull. After Armstrong and Cool stopped laughing and realized that something might actually be wrong, they called an ambulance. And thus was born the song's lyrical metaphor for heartache as actual physical pain.

The album was mixed in LA in late 1993, as the band members went home to catch up on their lives and rehearse for a short summer tour with pop-punk pioneers Bad Religion. Armstrong spent a lot of this time on the phone with Adrienne Nesser, back in Minnesota. His relationship with the punk rocker Amanda fell apart, thanks to the great "sellout" debate, and she left for Ecuador, saying she couldn't live in a world ruled by corporations. She never cared about any of Armstrong's later successes, but she fired the growing conflict within Armstrong that drove him to write, and her inspiration comes through in many later Green Day songs, like "Sassafras Roots," "Good Riddance," and "She's a Rebel." Once again, although they weren't together, Armstrong turned to Adrienne to talk things through. He convinced her to come visit between the Bad Religion tour and the album's release, when he thought he'd have some downtime. Downtime, though, became surprisingly rare surprisingly fast.

THE ART OF BUILDUP

"When I turned in the record the people at the company immediately said, 'Oh, we've got something here, guys," says Cavallo.[7] Reprise was ready to go all out on marketing for *Dookie*, but Green Day insisted on choosing how it represented itself to the world. The bandmates refused a cute pinup shot for the cover and enlisted East Bay fanzine artist Richie Bucher to design it instead. Even the marketing execs were behind the decision, knowing that they couldn't afford to disconnect this grassroots band completely from the subculture that had spawned it. "I think that they saw a fanzine cover for Eggplant's zine *Absolutely Zippo* and they liked it," Bucher recalls, "Billie Joe just told me that it was gonna be called *Dookie* so I had that to work with, the whole shit theme. That was all I really needed. I had just had this little germ of an idea, and I did a drawing—you know, with the plane coming down and swooping over and dropping shit. Then I saw characters around and just drew them in."[8] Nods to Ozzy Osbourne and Black Panther leader Huey P. Newton show up alongside a cartoon of Gilman's resident photographer Murray Bowles and graffiti referencing Berkeley punks Twisted Dog Sisters—and, of course, there are also a few dogs and monkeys throwing their own feces. In a mainstream culture currently dominated by grunge's darker aesthetic and Sub Pop Records's minimalist black and white album covers, *Dookie* was going to stand out.

Before the album was scheduled to hit stores, Green Day had to hit the road for their tour with Bad Religion. The older LA band had started mixing pop and punk years before Green Day came on the scene, even though Green Day later got the lion's share of credit (or blame) for the pop-punk explosion of the mid- to late-1990s that brought Blink-182, New Found Glory, Sum 41, and others to fame. At the time, it was intimidating to open for these elder statesmen, especially in California, where they had a large, loyal audience—but Green Day approached the tour with the same bratty swagger as always, and converted fans even in the heart of LA. After seeing how well the band went over, Warner Bros.'s marketing director Geoffrey Weiss said, "My goal was to have a successful record, which to me meant that if we sold a couple hundred thousand records, it would be fantastic. I remember when Rob was making the record, I asked Tré what his goal was. And he said, 'Oh, I just want to sell half a million copies,' which I thought at the time was a ridiculously ambitious thing to say."[9]

Armstrong snuck off for a quick tour with his side project Pinhead Gunpowder before *Dookie* came out, and reconnected with the scrappy life on tour that Green Day was rapidly leaving behind. "I wanted to experience as much from that tour as I could," he told Lawrence Livermore later. "We played Olympia [Washington]—Olympia had a really great scene at that time—and we were playing at the Lucky 7 house, and I just wanted to experience as much out of that as I could, because I felt like there was no turning back, that anything could happen. It was a crapshoot. And it was scary, thinking about what might be ahead. There was the punk scene, and what might happen to the punk scene, but at the same time, I was thinking about what the f*** is going to happen to my life."[10]

OUTSIDE PRESSURE

Armstrong may have had some control over his own life, but Green Day had no control over the direction of rock or the cultural moment that would greet them on *Dookie*'s release. The band members were coming from a working-class background and had believed all along that, because their music was good and deserved to be heard by as many people as possible, they would do whatever it took to realize their potential. This was an important difference between Green Day and the grunge craze that was currently weighing on Kurt Cobain's mind and sprouting all kinds of derivative second- and third-rate bands.

The apathetic, ironic members of Generation X, made famous through movies such as *Slacker* and *Singles*, were mostly white and middle-class, with the luxury of going to college. The members of Green Day hadn't grown up with the expectation that their parents would support them—in fact, as soon as they got the chance, they began supporting their parents. They knew what it was like to worry about rent and see your parents working graveyard shifts. "I did not realize until I talked to the Green Day guys at length that they came from far less advantaged backgrounds than most of the people in the punk underground and most of the more-radical-than-thou," says radical punk icon Jello Biafra, formerly of the Dead Kennedys.[11] It's easier to concentrate on abstract ideals and create restrictive rules around culture and art when you're not concerned with working for a living. Michael Azerrad used the working-class band the Minutemen as an example of this division in his seminal book *Our Band Could Be*

Your Life. "If you're working class," he writes, "you don't start a band to just scrape by; you start a band to get rich. So art bands, with their inherently limited commercial prospects, were mainly the province of the affluent."[12] From the beginning, Armstrong, Dirnt, and Cool aimed to support themselves through music, and they reached that goal early on—even if they were hanging on in filthy crash pads. When asked by a reporter at *Spin* if they still considered themselves working class, they bristled. "Armstrong: 'I definitely work my ass off.' Dirnt: 'We work super hard not to have to work.' Tré : 'We put in some serious f****** hours to be considered slackers.'"[13] They honestly believed that their band deserved recognition, and were prepared to do the work to get there. But they were about to enter Generation X's world, which overlapped with punk rock in the value it placed on credibility and its almost ascetic distaste for financial success.

DOOKIE HITS THE FAN

On February 1, 1994, *Dookie* was released on Reprise Records, and debuted at 127 in the Billboard Top 200 chart. The first shipment unexpectedly sold out, and Warner Bros. had to rush to ship more, creating a buzz as the wait lists grew longer. The single "Longview" came out the same day, fueling excitement for the release as modern rock radio and college radio put it in constant rotation. "*Dookie* was one of those records where we had to refrain from putting five songs on the radio [at once]," recalled K-ROQ music director Lisa Worden. "When we got the album it was like, 'Oh my God! Oh my God!' K-ROQ's famous for putting on too many things and the label freaks out and it just pulls us back. But we did put 'Basket Case' on right away too."[14]

The video for "Longview" followed shortly, directed by Mark Kohr, who had worked under Tim Burton and done several videos for another East Bay band, Primus. All the shooting took place in the band's basement apartment over two days. They stayed close to home mostly because they only had the budget to do a performance video, but it did help the band get the realistic look they were going for. "We had cultivated quite a few zits at that point," Dirnt told VH1 later. "Kinda cool."[15] Kohr only made a few changes: he painted the walls blue and red and brought in a monkey and a stunt couch for the climactic scene, where a bored Armstrong stabs the cushions with a bread knife because there's nothing good on TV. (The band wasn't making enough yet to justify ripping holes in their own couch.) "I love seeing that video, because it reminds me of what I saw when I first went down there," recalled Rob Cavallo. "It's exactly what I saw. We played some guitars and got stoned—where the camera is in the video is where I was sitting when I was first there."[16]

That authenticity and bravado came across to viewers, turning many into fans. "I came home from school one day, turned on MTV, and the 'Longview' video was the first video I saw," recalled Billy Martin of the band Good Charlotte. "I still had my backpack on and I was standing up. I couldn't sit down because I wanted to wait until the video was over. It was captivating."[17] In March, the band showed up on other TV shows, including MTV's *120 Minutes* and *The Jon Stewart Show*. On March 16, Green Day appeared on *Late Night with Conan O'Brien*, and, apparently, Dirnt wasn't happy with the way he looked or sounded. "The initial shock made me so mad, I was in a hotel room and started smashing lamps. I actually destroyed a hotel room," he admits. "It was stupid, but it wasn't a rock star thing to do."[18] That may seem like a strange spin on it—after all, trashing hotel rooms is one of the great rock clichés—but Dirnt wasn't yet a rich, entitled asshole; he was still a confused, angry suburban kid, so perhaps his evasion makes sense. At any rate, none of their confusion or anger slowed *Dookie*'s momentum.

POP CULTURE SHOCK

As the "Longview" video gained traction on MTV in the spring of 1994, grunge lost some of its creative momentum, and Nirvana in particular was spinning out of control. After a successful *MTV Unplugged* acoustic show in December, Nirvana went out on a spring tour of Europe. Kurt Cobain overdosed on prescription drugs and alcohol in Rome on March 4 and his wife, Courtney Love, rushed him to the hospital. The incident resulted in the tour being canceled and garnered international media attention. Cobain's heroin addiction reared its head again over the next few weeks: he went into rehab, and, less than a week later, hopped the fence and flew back to Seattle. About a week later, on Friday, April 8, Cobain was found dead of a self-inflicted shotgun wound to the head in his Seattle home.

"All of a sudden there was no one there," Armstrong recalled later. "It was like there was no leader anymore."[19] Cobain had always felt torn about the "voice of a generation" role that success had imposed on him, and the scrutiny only intensified after his death. Fans thronged his neighborhood that weekend, and 10,000 people gathered under the Space Needle on Sunday for a public memorial. Taped messages from Love and bassist Krist Novoselic were played; after Love's emotional words, Novoselic offered some hope for moving forward. He asked fans to remember that Cobain had an "ethic toward his fans that was rooted in the punk rock way of thinking: No band is special, no player royalty. If you've got a guitar and a lot of soul, just bang something out and mean it."[20]

In the vacuum that followed the despair of Cobain's death, Green Day had enough soul to change the mood. Just when the tortured poses of third-generation grunge went sour, these clowns popped up. As *Rolling Stone* put it, "Beavis and Butt-Head have started a band: It's called Green Day."[21] The cartoon album cover, the title that meant "poo-poo," and the colorful videos all worked together to attract kids of all ages (despite the fact that Sesame Street's Ernie had to be removed from the back cover for legal reasons). Green Day was eventually mocked for the number of nine-year-olds at their concerts, but they truly did have broad appeal. They hadn't given up on angst altogether, with songs about lethargy, cynicism, resentment, and love gone wrong—but they showed it in a loud, dumb, funny way. "Longview" made it to MTV's Buzz Bin, which pushed the single to the top of the Billboard Modern Rock chart as radio stations across the country picked it up.

SPAWNING THE NEXT GENERATION

Green Day wasn't alone in its success: it just opened the gates for the next wave of punk. In April, Brett Gurewitz of Bad Religion released an album by the Orange County punk band The Offspring on his well-known independent label Epitaph Records. The Offspring had often played Gilman on West Coast tours, and had already been to Europe supporting NOFX. Their first album, *Ignition*, sold about 45,000 copies (comparable to *Kerplunk!*) but Gurewitz didn't have any particular expectations for their new album, *Smash*. The band sent him the mixes as soon as they were ready, and he popped the album into his car stereo on the way home. "I couldn't believe what I was hearing," he recalled. "I didn't drive straight home that day. I drove round and round the block, just listening to the music. Two songs in particular grabbed my attention, 'Come Out and Play' and 'Low Self Esteem.' I had all these thoughts flying through my head as I was driving around. And when I did finally get home I walked into the house and said to my then-wife Maggie, 'Hi honey, we're going to be rich!' She said, 'That's nice dear—dinner's ready!'"[22] Gurewitz had it right: he tapped "Come Out and Play" as the album's first single, and radio and MTV grabbed ahold of it as quickly as they had latched onto "Longview."

As with Nirvana and Pearl Jam a few years earlier, one hit single is a fluke, but two bands with shared roots is a movement. "It felt that what Nirvana was to grunge, Green Day was to the new punk movement," said K-ROQ program director Kevin Weatherly. "Obviously, there were some punk bands in the '80s but they never really broke out of that. Being kind of defined as just a punk band. *These* were punk bands that really wrote big, fat hit songs."[23]

Epitaph had been hanging by a thread before the Offspring blew up, but now they had a few aces up their sleeve. Another of their bands, Rancid, included two former members of the iconic Gilman band Operation Ivy, Tim Armstrong and Matt Freeman, along with Brett Reed on drums. They had put out one album on Lookout! before signing to Epitaph and knew the members of Green Day—in fact, Billie Joe Armstrong co-wrote the song "Radio, Radio" with Freeman and Tim Armstrong, and he played one show with them before Lars Frederiksen came on board in 1993. (Rumor has it that Billie Joe was invited to join Rancid, but decided to stick with Green Day.) Their 1994 record *Let's Go*, which included "Radio, Radio," rode the Green Day-created wave to number 97 on the Billboard Top 200 chart. The Offspring also took Rancid on tour that year. Their combination of gritty realism and sing-along choruses was ready for its moment in the sun, and they wouldn't have to wait long. In 1995, they released . . . *And Out Come the Wolves*, which went gold the next year and has since been certified platinum. Singles such as "Ruby SoHo" and "Time Bomb" helped create a bridge between punk and ska in the mid-1990s, when bands of both types were popping up like magic mushrooms.

PICKING UP THE PACE

Despite the initial surprising sales and response surrounding *Dookie* in 1994, Green Day had a lot of work to do still. They headed out in late April for a European tour, playing forty shows across the

UK, Belgium, Denmark, Holland, Italy, Spain, and Sweden. In Germany, for the first time since their squatter shows, they found themselves in a very different situation, opening nine arena shows for Die Toten Hosen in front of ten thousand people every night. Rob Cavallo flew in and met the band in Spain to record shows for later use as live B-sides—and also to document a band and a live show that was rapidly evolving. He went with the band to London, where the tour began and ended, to record a BBC Radio session at the Maida Vale studios.

Cavallo was there to meet the band when they got home in June, and broke some news. "I picked them up at the airport, and I got them all in a rental car and said to them, 'Guys, I gotta tell you something, you know, all the indicators point to the fact that you're gonna sell a couple a million records even though we've only sold a couple hundred thousand or two hundred and fifty thousand. Just the trajectory of the single, all the research a record company can do is telling us that it's gonna be pretty f***** huge.' And Tré, who I love, says to me, 'Well of course it is, Rob. What did you expect?' And I said, 'Yeah, but I think it's bigger than you even think. And it's bigger than we ever thought.' There was silence for the first five or ten seconds. They were letting it sink in. And then we just started hopping and hollering and having a great time."[24] Even though they were all thrilled, as anyone would be, they took a second to absorb the full meaning of such success before celebrating.

The effect of *Dookie*'s release on the band members' lives was unpredictable and disruptive. None of them were more than twenty-two years old at the time—they talked about trying to get into the bar scene and being recognized, people wanting to make friends, start fights, ask questions. The schmoozers began to close in just as the punk rock community abandoned them.

Around this time, Armstrong decided that he couldn't wait any longer to be with Adrienne Nesser. She had been managing a Pier 1 Imports store in Minnesota after graduating from college, and he convinced her to move to California. Then, a month later, they impulsively decided to get married in his backyard. "I was really nervous, so I started pounding beers," Armstrong said, "and so did Adrienne. The ceremony lasted five minutes. Neither of us are any religion, so we pieced together speeches. One Catholic, one Protestant, one Jewish. It was a lot of fun. Then we went to the Claremont Hotel, and we f***** like bunnies."[25] Armstrong has said many times that the wedding was a crazy impulsive decision, but neither of them regrets it. As Green Day's fame grew, he needed some kind of grounding in real life—and he got it all at once. The very next day, to their delight, they found out Adrienne was pregnant. "I think he felt untethered," Armstrong's sister Anna says. "And Adrienne was somebody he could put in his pocket in a lot of ways. He could carry his family or someone close to him with him at all times. He loved her and he knew that she loved him. I think when he was feeling alone she made him feel that he wasn't."[26] They bought a house in north Berkeley to prepare for the baby, but after a fan announced their address on local radio, fans started crowding the yard. The couple was forced to sell the house and move to preserve their privacy.

Mike Dirnt and Tré Cool followed a very similar path: Cool's girlfriend Lisea Lyon got pregnant soon after Armstrong and Nesser's wedding, and, a little while later, Dirnt married his longtime girlfriend Anastacia. As the pressure mounted and they found themselves constantly on the road, the band members felt a real need to step up in their relationships as well as their work.

THE MONEY QUESTION

Ever since Green Day signed to a major label, punk rockers and former fans had accused them of selling out and made it clear they had burned their bridges with their old community. The band couldn't ignore the animosity in the air. *Maximumrocknroll*, the local magazine the band grew up respecting, never tired of publishing harsh opinions of Green Day, and the band didn't always rise above the pressure—they were defensive in interviews and sensitive to insinuations that they were greedy rock stars. Armstrong provided for his mother, although she didn't want to leave the house she had raised her family in—she still lives there. But sports cars and bling never entered the picture. These guys had grown up couch-surfing and sleeping in the bookmobile, and didn't jump at the chance to change the way they lived. "I set my life up so I could be happy regardless of what my income was," Dirnt told *Rolling Stone*. "If you can set up a lifestyle where you can always be happy—mine was around musicians and friends—and have no other expectations, then anything else that happens is icing on the cake."[27]

To live up to the Gilman Street ethics that they carried with them and prove that they really weren't in it for the money, Green Day worked to keep ticket prices down for their shows, although they were selling out arenas now and could have charged rock star prices. Grunge superstars Pearl Jam had started a well-publicized feud with Ticketmaster, refusing to play any venue that used the monopolistic service and limiting their tour options in the process. Green Day took a different tack, choosing to keep ticket prices down by lowering their own percentage instead of getting into a drawn-out fight with Ticketmaster. "We don't give a f*** about Ticketmaster. We're charging what we're worth, and we don't think we're worth $22.50. We take a lower cut than Pearl Jam. I'm not picking on them, I'm just saying that to anyone in general who's complaining about it."[28] With a bare-bones road crew and bunks on the tour bus instead of fancy hotels, the band kept tickets down as low as $5 or $7. They also lost money in the process—contrary to the conventional wisdom that bands make most of their money on tour and only a small part from album sales, Green Day lost something like $15,000 on their summer tour.

A few key appearances later in the summer helped make up the loss: on August 5, Green Day joined the Lollapalooza tour as the opening act, replacing Japanese experimental noise-punks the Boredoms. The Smashing Pumpkins headlined the festival instead of scheduled headliner Nirvana, who broke up after Kurt Cobain's tragic suicide. Other bands included mainstream bands like the Beastie Boys and Cypress Hill, as well as alt-rockers the Breeders, the Flaming Lips, and Guided By Voices. While these groups had strong followings of their own, none had risen as quickly or as recently as Green Day, who found themselves in a strange position as the hottest act on the bill. Fans rushed the gates at every tour stop to catch Green Day's noon shows, straining the festival's resources.

Even the most well-organized staff couldn't have survived the next festival Green Day played. They secured their status as an important part of the music world when the organizers of Woodstock '94 invited them to play one weekend in August for an estimated 300,000 people and a pay-per-view audience in the millions. Some people wanted Green Day to take the opportunity, and some thought they should stay out of it. After all, the original Woodstock, in 1969, had nothing to do with punk past or present, and Green Day so clearly belonged to their own time. Would it really be a good idea for them to appear alongside Bob Dylan, Peter Gabriel, and Santana—not to mention corporate sponsors Pepsi, Haagen-Dazs, and Apple? The answer, from an economic perspective, was yes. (From a health and sanity standpoint, though, the answer was probably different.) Dirnt freely admitted in *Time* that Woodstock "is really corporate.

But that's one of the reasons we're playing. It's helping us make up a lot of the money we've lost touring, being out there keeping our ticket prices low."[29] Nobody could have known that Green Day's Sunday afternoon show would become the best-remembered moment of the whole festival, but a lot of people were waiting for them by the time 3:00 p.m. rolled around on that rainy Sunday. The musicians who came on right before Green Day's set all came from Peter Gabriel's WOMAD world music festival, and, needless to say, failed to captivate Green Day's fans. The crowd, milling about in what had become an 850-acre mud pit, alternately booed and chanted Green Day's name through the WOMAD set.

By the time Green Day came on stage the audience was impatient and covered in mud. They opened with "Welcome to Paradise," and someone must not have appreciated the irony, because a few handfuls of mud hit the stage. "Come on you assholes, throw some more!" Armstrong yelled, and stuck a clump of dirt in his mouth.[30] The slop started flying, covering the entire stage and clogging up all the instruments. Armstrong dropped the mike and started flinging clods back into the crowd. Dirnt lay down in the muck, all the while keeping the bassline in time with Cool, as Armstrong dropped his pants on pay-per-view television and taunted the crowd. Fans kept rushing the stage, climbing over the safety barriers. Finally, Armstrong asked the crowd to shout "Shut the f*** up!" When they did, the band walked out. In the chaos after their set, one panicked security guard mistook a mud-crusted Dirnt for a fan and tackled him, slamming his face down on a monitor and knocking out several of his teeth. It got so bad that the whole group had to escape by helicopter.

For a festival that seemed like one big marketing gimmick, Green Day's set provided some refreshingly honest idiocy. "I went in there with low expectations and came out overwhelmed," Armstrong told the *Los Angeles Times* a few weeks later. "It was the closest thing to chaos, and complete anarchy, that I have ever seen in my whole life."[31] Dirnt added, "It took me a few days to stop thinking about it."[32] Cool, on the other hand, relished the anarchy (maybe because he was shielded behind the drums). "It was amazing!" he said later. "I look back on it now and it still makes me smile—all that mud, that chaos and trouble."[33]

Despite the angry letter Armstrong's mother sent him, calling him "disrespectful and indecent,"[34] the band had many reasons to smile after Woodstock. The next week, *Dookie* shot to number 5 on the Billboard charts, eventually peaking at number 2. Their publicity team couldn't answer the phones fast enough to respond to all the interview requests from American and foreign journalists. In one afternoon, Green Day shattered the barriers between punk and the mainstream: they were now household names.

With perfect timing, the "Basket Case" single and video came out that same month, and the public ate it up. Green Day interrupted their tour to perform at the MTV Video Music Awards and nailed a frantic performance, although "Longview" didn't win any of the three awards it was nominated for. They had better luck at the Billboard Music Video Awards, and took home their first trophy ever, for Best New Artist Clip of the Year.

The accolades didn't last long, though: less than a month after the Woodstock debacle, Green Day were back in trouble. On September 9, the band scheduled a free concert in the Hatch Shell at the Boston Opera House, sponsored by local rock station WFNS. The radio station anticipated a rowdy scene, but they were caught completely off guard when more than 100,000 people showed up. The crowd chanted for Green Day throughout the opening set by the Meices, and several announcements between sets failed to calm the crowd down. The security team, composed of police, state troopers, and fifteen inmates from the local prison, threatened to shut down the show if things didn't settle down—the crowd responded with chants of "Pigs suck!" and "Hell no, we won't go!" The band finally began their set, but less than half an hour later, Armstrong got caught up in the moment during "Longview" and jumped off the stage into a flowerbed and started ripping it up. That was it: fearing that the entire lighting rig would collapse, the cops shut off the power. The crowd went nuts, bottles started flying, and the mayhem spread into the streets. "The police were getting beat up and stuff," said Tré. "They were tear-gassing the crowd and all these things."[35] From a safe distance, the band watched the chaos while signing autographs for the prisoners on security duty. The arrests and injuries dominated local news, with damages to the building estimated at $20,000.

It seemed like the perfect time to get out of town; the band went off to Europe for three weeks. They came back in time to start yet another U.S. tour, bringing Germany's Die Toten Hosen back with them and inviting the self-proclaimed "queercore" band and Lookout! signees Pansy Division to open. Green Day selected Pansy Division, whose members were mostly gay, to make the point that their roots still mattered, and that they wouldn't shy away from challenging their audiences with radical politics. With bigger shows came broader audiences, who might not take kindly to songs like "James

Bondage" and "Rock & Roll Queer Bar." If people didn't like it, they could just leave. And if they tried to ignore it, the band wouldn't let them. "The funny thing was watching some of these guys in the audience when Pansy Division opened," Armstrong remembered. "They were out there flexing their muscles and acting real macho, not really realizing that Pansy Division is gay. Then Chris Freeman, Pansy's bass player, would stop in the middle of a song and say, 'So, have you guys figured out we're a bunch of fags yet?' I think Pansy Division is the kind of band that saves people's lives. They're catchy, and they're really educational. They're honest about their sexuality, and that saves lives."[36] Back in the early '90s, it wasn't easy to be so honest. 1994 was the first year that doctors publicly denounced treatments designed to "cure" homosexuality, but gay people still weren't as widely accepted as they became over the next fifteen years. They certainly couldn't get married or have any of the rights married heterosexuals automatically enjoyed.

Partly in solidarity with the movement Pansy Division represented, Armstrong gave a candid, revealing interview to *The Advocate* soon after the tour and discussed his own sexuality. "I think I've always been bisexual," he said simply. "I mean, it's something that I've always been interested in. I think everybody kind of fantasizes about the same sex. I think people are born bisexual, and it's just that our parents and society kind of veer us off into this feeling of *Oh, I can't.* They say it's taboo. It's ingrained in our heads that it's bad, when it's not bad at all. It's a very beautiful thing."[37] He went on to say that he'd never acted on those feelings, but he had struggled with sexuality, particularly in high school when macho boys insulted each other and started fights by making insinuations about others' sexuality. One of his uncles was also gay, and battling AIDS at the time, so these issues hit home for Armstrong. On December 3, they played at a fundraising event to combat AIDS, LIFEbeat's CounterAid benefit. This was one of the first of the many benefits they would go on to play—and they did it the same day they performed on *Saturday Night Live.*

HOMETOWN BOOM

In a lot of ways, Green Day's success with *Dookie* benefited the Gilman Street scene, despite Gilman's rejection of the band members. Whereas *39/Smooth* and *Kerplunk!* had sold thousands of copies a month when Green Day were signed to Lookout!, the current sales went far beyond that. Their total sales shot up, from hundreds of thousands of dollars a year to millions, as fans discovered Green Day's back catalog and other bands from the Gilman scene. Some purists at Gilman started saying that bands on Lookout! were too big-time to play Gilman, or had outgrown the venue, but no action was ever taken—it was just another case of insular punks pushing for arcane new rules about credibility.

The club itself benefited monetarily, starting in about 1992 and continuing for years as its fame spread, thanks to Green Day and Rancid. They were able to pay their back rent and fix up the most trashed parts of the club. "Ever since Rodeo's own Green Day became a multi-platinum-selling band last year," the local paper reported, "you can't pick up a copy of *Rolling Stone*, *Spin*, or other mainstream magazines without some mention of the 600-person, general admission venue a few miles west of the UC-Berkeley campus. This collective, run solely by volunteers, has become one of the meccas of the punk-rock revival. Bands from Japan, Hawaii, England and the Czech Republic are playing there now, along with local punkers cutting their teeth. Foreigners stop by in mid-afternoon just to see the place."[38]

Gilman's fame has continued ever since then, and bills with four or even five small local bands still fill the club on weekends. Green Day made a donation to Gilman in 2007, according to old friend and Berkeley activist Jesse Townley. He didn't see their move to a major label as a betrayal of their own deep convictions; in fact, they never upheld the idea of "punk rock being an exclusive 'f*** you, we'll never sell out'" genre, because of their working-class suburban roots. "I think Green Day never bought 100 percent into that," he said. "Just from their background they were like, yeah, it would be great if we could sell out the [Oakland] Coliseum. However, they didn't think they would ever do it."[39]

HAPPY NEW YEAR

Years later, it was still hard for Green Day to believe that they were selling out arenas. As Dirnt said in *Rolling Stone*, "Someone said to me before a show the other day, 'Fifteen thousand people at this arena—this is everything you ever dreamed of.' I turned to him and said, 'Correction. It's everything I *never* dreamed of.'"[40] But it had happened this way all year, all over the country, and Green Day wasn't done yet. Its last major concert of 1994 was the Acoustic Christmas Concert at Madison Square Garden, hosted by New York radio station Z100. The lineup featured Bon Jovi, Sheryl Crow, Hole, Indigo Girls, Weezer, and more—but, once again, Green Day stood out from the crowd. Armstrong popped up at 2:00 a.m. for an encore performance of "She" completely naked except his strategically placed guitar. A few days later, Armstrong told *Entertainment Weekly*, "I'm just exhausted. Totally. We've outdone ourselves in a serious way. I have insomnia problems anyway, so it's hard for me to sleep. That's the main thing I'm looking forward to: I'll probably sleep the rest of the year."[41]

The new year came and went in a flurry of honors and excitement. In January, the band appeared on the cover of *Rolling Stone*, as the recipients of the magazine's award for Best New Band. That same month, "When I Come Around" became the third single from *Dookie*. The band stuck to their guns and refused to do a video or single release for "Welcome to Paradise" next, despite its huge popularity on the radio, because it felt too strange to re-record a song that evocative of their past.

In March, Armstrong hit two major milestones: his first Grammy and his first child. The Grammy was awarded to *Dookie* for Best Alternative Music Performance—Sheryl Crow beat them for Best New Artist. Armstrong and Nesser allegedly named little Joseph Marciano Armstrong after punk rocker Joey Ramone and boxer Rocky Marciano. This seems more likely when you consider the name of their second child, Jakob, born in 1998: Danger is his middle name. Cool had married his girlfriend Lisea Lyon, and their daughter Ramona (possibly also named for Joey Ramone) was born in January. At the beginning of 1994, Green Day was a quickly growing club act, the members were all single, and they hoped their new record would pay the bills. By the end of the year, they had sold out arenas, found stable relationships, and sold millions of records. "We had been told, and it had been proved many times, that you can't sell punk rock and there will never be a big punk rock record," Cool recalled. "We blew that myth out of the water." Not bad for a bunch of punks.

NOTES

1. Marc Spitz, *Nobody Likes You: Inside the Turbulent Life, Times, and Music of Green Day* (New York: Hyperion, 2006), 85-86.

2. Ben Myers, *Green Day: American Idiots and the New Punk Explosion* (New York: The Disinformation Company, Inc. 2006), 103.

3. Spitz, 92.

4. Steven Rosen, "Green Day," *Total Guitar Bass Special*, Fall 2004, 28.

5. Myers, 98.

6. Spitz, 93.

7. Ibid., 96.

8. Ibid., 97.

9. Ibid., 99.

10. Lawrence Livermore, "Lawrence Livermore Interview," http://greenday.net/livermore.htm (accessed December 10, 2008).

11. Spitz, 90.

12. Michael Azerrad, *Our Band Could Be Your Life: Scenes from the American Indie Underground 1981-1991* (New York: Back Bay Books, 2002), 62.

13. Craig Marks, "An American Family," *Spin*, December 1995, 61.

14. Spitz, 104.

15. Mike Dirnt, quoted in "Green Day," *VH1 Behind the Music*, 2002.

16. Myers, 106.

17. Joe D'Angelo, "How Green Day's *Dookie* Fertilized a Punk-Rock Revival," http://www.mtv.com/news/articles/1491001/20040915/green_day.jhtml (accessed December 4, 2008).

18. Jeff Gordinier, "It's Not Easy Being Green Day," *Entertainment Weekly*, June 10, 1994.

19. Spitz, 101.

20. Gene Stout, "A Message of Love, Grief for Cobain," *The Seattle Post-Intelligencer*, Monday, April 11, 1004, A1. Also: Clark Humphrey, "Kurt Cobain, Seven Years Later," http://www.historylink.org/index.cfm?DisplayPage=output.cfm&File_Id=3263 (accessed December 4, 2008).

21. Doug Small, *Omnibus Press Presents the Story of: Green Day* (New York: Omnibus Press, 2005), 25.

22. Myers, 117.

23. Spitz, 103-104.

24. Ibid.,105.

25. Mundy, 37.

26. Spitz, 106.

27. Small, 37.

28. Alec Foege, "Green Day," *Rolling Stone*, December 28, 1995–January 11, 1996, 49.

29. Christopher John Farley, "Woodstock Suburb," *Time*, August 22, 1994, http://www.time.com/time/magazine/article/0,9171,981316-1,00.html (accessed March 15, 2009).

30. Spitz, 112.

31. Steve Appleford, "An Endless Summer for Green Day," *Los Angeles Times*, September 6, 1994, 1.

32. Ibid.
33. Myers, 111.
34. Mundy, 36.
35. Myers, 112.
36. Judy Wieder, "Coming Clean: Woodstock '94 star Billie Joe of Green Day goes triple platinum and lines up with the pansies," *The Advocate*, January 24, 1995.
37. Ibid.
38. Joe Garofoli, "Hard-Core Heaven," *West County Times*, December 27, 1995, 1F.
39. Rajesh Srinivasan, "Best Thing In Town," *The Daily Californian*, December 1, 2008.
40. Mundy, 39.
41. Small, 33.

CHAPTER FIVE

Walking Contradiction

Despite the accolades, the cash, and their growing families, the members of Green Day felt shell-shocked by the reaction to *Dookie*, both positive and negative. Music had been the one stable thing in their lives for so long, and now it had escaped their control. No matter the quality of the songs, the enthusiasm of mainstream fans for their music meant that the old fans and friends rejected the same music. "I couldn't find the strength to convince myself that what I was doing was a good thing," Billie Joe Armstrong said later. "I was in a band that was huge because it was supposed to be huge, because our songs were that good. I couldn't ever feel like I was doing the right thing, because it felt like I was making so many people angry. That's where I got so confused, and it became really stupid. I would never want to live that part of my life over again. Ever."[1] Unsure how to enjoy their success, they retreated a bit; they became more defensive in interviews and gave off an angrier vibe, which came through in the songs they wrote during this period. On top of everything else, Billie Joe spent many sleepless nights taking care of his infant son while trying out song ideas; the resulting record was eventually titled *Insomniac*.

Once again, in tough times the three friends pulled closer to each other: Billie Joe Armstrong, Mike Dirnt, and Tré Cool all bought houses in the suburbs outside Oakland in early 1995. Even though they finally could have escaped the suburbs that bored them as teenagers, they chose to hang on to familiarity as the rest of their world grew more and more strange. Despite spending more time near them, Armstrong didn't even let his mother and siblings talk about his success around him—the topic was off limits. Tré married his girlfriend Lisea Lyon in March, and the band took an official hiatus to spend time with family and write songs. This didn't exactly alleviate their responsibilities—they became more and more aware of what it takes to raise kids. "Being a parent is the hardest thing I've ever had to do in my whole life," Armstrong told *Spin* in a band interview. "I'm totally self-conscious all the time, making sure I don't scream in front of Joey, trying to keep some sort of comfortable atmosphere for him. I'm not used to that. I'm usually like 'arrrgghh!'" Tré added, "You can't just pull out the gun and blow away the telly anymore when there's something on you don't like, 'cause the baby might be sleeping."[2]

MONEY FOR NOTHING?

By now the word was out that a new album would be released in the fall, even though the band hadn't even finished writing the songs. The new Green Day album was the most anticipated release of 1995, along with the Smashing Pumpkins double disc *Mellon Collie and the Infinite Sadness*. At home, the band got recognized all over town; people asked about the album in grocery stores and coffee shops. Reacting to their loss of privacy, the bandmates closed ranks. They went out rarely, and they brought friends on board as assistants and techs, like Bill Schneider, the band's current tour manager and a longtime member of Pinhead Gunpowder.

At this point, nobody had any sympathy for the problems of the three "rock stars," but they still felt stung by the assumptions people made about them. They weren't the kind of stars who reveled in conspicuous consumption—they were still working-class punks at heart and they wanted people to see that. There's a big difference between their earlier clowning interviews in fanzines like *Flipside* and their prickly interviews in big magazines in 1995 and 1996. "One question we get asked a lot now," Dirnt said in *Spin*, "is 'How much money do you make?' When I was younger, I actually asked that question to my mom's friend. My mom took me and slapped me in the face and said 'Do *not* ask that question. It's none of your business.' Sure, we make money. We make plenty of money. And it's peace of mind for me to know that I've bought my mom a house and that my little sisters don't have to live in a trailer anymore."[3] They spent money on family and not that much else. "I have the same car," Armstrong said in November 1995. "I drive a Ford Fairlane, and I got it primered. That was about it."[4]

The trio continued practicing in an Oakland garage, and kept an eye out for ways to use their success to help others. On May 27 and 28, 1995, Green Day played two benefit shows at the Henry J. Kaiser Auditorium in Oakland. The proceeds went to the San Francisco Coalition on Homelessness, the Berkeley Free Clinic, the Haight-Ashbury Free Clinic, and Food Not Bombs, a decidedly punk rock organization whose members dumpster-dive for usable food and host meals for the homeless in public places to protest rampant waste in society. Green Day often pointed to these benefits later in their career to prove that their Gilman Street ethics remained intact.

With all their concerns about their image and proving to themselves and the world that they could still rock after making it big, the members of Green Day went into the studio in the summer of 1995 ready to make *Insomniac* darker than anything they had done before. Although they had very rarely ventured to the harder end of the punk spectrum before, they now found themselves in the position of representing punk rock to the masses, which only added to the pressure.

BACK TO BASICS

Before they finished *Insomniac*, they recorded a single for the soundtrack of the teen movie *Angus*: "J.A.R.," named for Jason Andrew Relva, a childhood friend who died in a car crash at age nineteen. In Relva's memory, Dirnt got the same tattoo that his friend had: a snake wrapped around a dagger, inscribed with the word "brother." The song itself is catchy and hopeful, with lyrics about choosing the kind of life you want to live, and it went over well on the radio. The problem was that the song reached the influential station K-ROQ much sooner than the band had planned—and they blamed their managers.

Elliot Cahn and Jeff Saltzmann had represented Green Day as managers and lawyers since the *Kerplunk!* days, but this was the first time the band had suspected them of going behind their backs. The pair had recently started their own record label, 510 Records, and, as the music supervisors for the *Angus* soundtrack, they got a few of their own bands on the album. (Green Day also helped get Pansy Division and Lookout! bands Tilt and the Riverdales on the soundtrack.) Green Day accused Cahn and Saltzman of putting their label first in leaking Green Day's song ahead of time. The rumor was that they had given out early copies to entice K-ROQ to play more songs from bands on 510 Records. It's not clear whether Cahn and Saltzmann were actually guilty as charged, but Green Day fired them anyway. "We felt like we weren't being treated as people anymore, but as assets," said Armstrong. "And so we were just like, 'F*** this.' We'll never have a corporate manager again."[5] The band may have also worried that their managers were bringing down their credibility; using the 510 area code of Oakland as their label name was kind of tacky, not to mention the corporate structure they were bringing to the band.

Whatever the reason, the band returned to their do-it-yourself roots in order to seize control in an out-of-control situation. They officially became self-managed, with their guitar tech Randy Steffes acting as their liaison. "The only three people who know what's best for Green Day are me, Billie, and Tré," Dirnt said.[6]

Cahn and Saltzman still had four years to go on their contract, though. Just a few days after "J.A.R." hit number 1 on the Billboard Modern Rock charts, knocking out Alanis Morissette's song "You Oughta Know," Cahn and Saltzman filed a lawsuit on August 29 demanding $165,000 in back wages from the band, plus 20% of future earnings for the next four years—a royalty rate the band disputed. Elliot Cahn claimed to be blindsided and knew of no reasons why the band members might have severed ties, but, as Green Day's lawyer Bernard Burk told the *San Francisco Chronicle*, "If he didn't see the road signs, he was driving with his eyes closed."[7] The management company didn't succeed in bleeding the band dry, and Green Day continued down their path as stubbornly as ever.

INSOMNIA'S NOT EASY ON THE EYES

As part of the band's effort to distance itself from the pop image they had acquired thanks to *Dookie*'s antics, they commissioned a piece of art for the cover titled "God Told Me to Skin You Alive." The artist, Winston Smith, came from the East Bay punk scene and knew Tré Cool from his Gilman days. Cool and Armstrong, along with producer Rob Cavallo, went over to Smith's house to go through his artwork, and ran into a prime example of how cut off they had become from their old community. "We went out for a pizza and looked at different stuff," Smith recalled, "and at one point I asked, 'So how's it going? You guys got a day job or did you sell any records for your last record?' You know, 'cause I had never seen their names all the time in *MRR*; all I could see was other bands in the Bay Area playing here and there. And he [Cool] says very calmly, 'Well, you know, our last record sold about nine million copies.' I nearly fell down. I thought they had printed them up and were peddling them out of the back of the VW microbus."[8] *Maximumrocknroll* carried absolutely no word of Green Day after they signed to a major label; it was possible to go two years in the East Bay without hearing anything about them.

That strangeness comes through in the raw art that Green Day chose to represent the album: a fold-out collage featuring flames, dental work, circus monkeys, and three skulls. (The third image is hidden: hold the artwork at an angle and a piece of wood poking out of the fire morphs into a skull.) The title came from a fake religious tract that Smith had created for a poster that came with the classic Dead Kennedys album *Fresh Fruit for Rotting Vegetables*.

CAN'T LOOK AWAY

In August, the band previewed songs from *Insomniac* on a European tour that included England's famed Reading festival, a massive outdoor concert headlined by the Smashing Pumpkins. The lead single, "Geek Stink Breath," came out on September 25, a couple of weeks before the album's release. With its heavy, stomping chords and chorus of "I'm picking scabs off my face," the song introduced a new, far less kid-friendly approach. It's all about the consequences of tweaking out on cheap crystal methamphetamine—clearly the band's attempt to avoid getting pinned down as harmless goofballs. The video turned it up a few more notches. The band brought back Mark Kohr as a director and had him film while a friend of Armstrong's who had a long history of drug abuse (and a sweet tooth) got his teeth pulled out at the dentist. The graphic images of a dentist yanking out a bloody tooth may have been nauseating, but they definitely made a point. "It's an ugly song for an ugly drug," Dirnt said. "We have a lot of friends hooked on speed. They're so tweaked out, man, it's ridiculous."[9]

Even though he had given up meth by the time the video was filmed, Armstrong wouldn't take a stand on whether meth users should stop. Of the song, he said, "It just describes a state of mind, and the destructiveness it had on me personally."[10] After the East Bay punk scene got national attention, it went through a period of increasing drug use, from pot to speed to heroin. Although the guys in Green Day made it out, some of their friends did not. Lucky Dog, the bassist for the Gilman band Fifteen, was one of those who took it further than partying and sank deeper and deeper into addiction until he died. Armstrong could still remember why the drug appealed to him at first, though: "I liked speed because I wanted some rocket fuel. I wanted to *think*. That's the difference between us and the grunge scene. We wanted to go *faster*."[11]

FAME AND FRUSTRATION

For a punk band, Green Day was undeniably huge. The only band that came close to their stature at this point was the Offspring. But despite still feeling like an underground band, when *Insomniac* came out on October 10, 1995, Green Day had entered an entirely different arena, competing against top-selling mainstream acts like Mariah Carey and Hootie and the Blowfish. Many reviewers compared *Insomniac* to Nirvana's album *In Utero*: both were identity-crisis albums that sprang from the shock of a breakout album's mainstream success (*Dookie* for Green Day and *Nevermind* for Nirvana). Green Day hadn't changed much musically, but the tone was different—it was more nihilistic, frustrated, and disillusioned. Some fans didn't buy into this, given Green Day's huge success—what did they have to complain about?

Of course, money and fame create as many problems as they solve. Green Day felt immense pressure for *Insomniac* to reach the same heights as *Dookie*, and it inevitably fell short. Despite debuting high on the charts and reaching number 2 on the Billboard 200 much faster than *Dookie* had, sales were far below those of the earlier album. By the end of the year, *Insomniac* had gone double platinum, something that would shock almost any other punk band, but that fell flat with Green Day. The band had succeeded in making an album with less pop appeal, and made no apologies for it. As Armstrong said, looking back in 1997, "It did a lot better than I thought it was going to do. We were prepared for what people were going to say. From the sound of it, we knew it wasn't going to sell as much as *Dookie*. . . . It had a sort of one-track mind. It was very aggressive through the whole thing. It was relentless."[12]

The band couldn't help but be a little stung by the album's relatively cool reception—remember, this was a band that had never denied their ambition and had always been confident in their songs and their playing. The problem of their image wasn't resolved by releasing this harder-edged album, either, although fans got a fuller picture. Perhaps as a result of its ongoing internal conflicts, Green Day made negative comments about other bands in interviews. On the other hand, they had always been brats.

Luckily, the record company had enough faith in the band—and the album did well enough—that they never actually got into financial trouble. "We were going after artists who we believed in, who have a vision that we can buy into and who we can help," said Howie Klein, the president of Reprise at the time. "Coming off this gigantic record *Dookie*, would we have liked to sell more records? Sure. But their work was not suffering. . . . Not for one second did I lose a nano-millimeter's worth of faith in Green Day."[13] It probably helped lift some of the pressure off Reprise and Green Day when Alanis Morissette's album *Jagged Little Pill* emerged soon after as the next Warner-affiliated blockbuster.

Even though Green Day currently held the title of biggest punk band in the world, by 1995 the punk world had headed down several different paths. The Offspring was also having an identity crisis, working on the follow-up to the multi-platinum *Smash*, the more hard-rock "sophomore slump" album *Ixnay on the Hombre*. Rancid shook off Madonna's label, Maverick, during a major-label bidding war, but ended up sticking with its independent label, Epitaph. The album Rancid released after that ordeal, . . . *And Out Come the Wolves*, stuck closer to traditional rabble-rousing punk rock than Green Day's more pop approach. It scored them three hit singles and MTV airplay and then went gold in six months. NOFX took an even more underground approach with their release *Punk in Drublic*: they refused to allow MTV to air their videos and did interviews only with respected fanzines. Their irreverent sense of humor, combined with Green Day's pop sensibility and ambition, proved to be an important influence on pop punk bands to come. For the moment, though, Green Day was still essentially the lone punk band on the national stage.

Armstrong insisted that he still had plenty of things to write angry, defiant songs about, even if he wasn't struggling with the same issues of a few years ago. He cited police brutality and racism as the larger issues that fired him up, but also emphasized the fact that his personal problem weren't over by any means: "There's things that piss me off every single day. As soon as you get rid of certain kinds of problems, like financial burdens and struggling, you inherit something completely different. I think a lot of the songs on the new record, I'm trying to define what I'm feeling and I'm trying to break it down to the core of that emotion."[14]

One of the most defiant (and most talked-about) songs on *Insomniac*, "86," deals with the emotions that came from 924 Gilman Street shutting its doors to Green Day and its members. Even though the ban was technically on major-label bands playing shows, the members of Green Day knew they were no longer welcome at the venue, even as fans: they had been 86'd, or banned. The song bluntly asserts the unwritten rule, "There's no return from 86." Once you leave the underground, there's no coming back. In a moment of perfect irony, they performed "86" on *Late Night with David Letterman*.

The next single, "Stuck With Me," didn't sell as well as Green Day and the label hoped it would, but they pressed on with touring. The band often brought their families along on tour, which led to some not-exactly-punk moments. At one show at London's Brixton Academy, the band insisted on starting their headlining set at 8:15 p.m., a ridiculously early time. With their families along, they told the crowd, they wanted to read their kids bedtime stories. Clearly, the tour was no longer their first priority.

The Green Day machine got a much-needed shot in the arm in early 1996, when the single "Brain Stew," backed with "Jaded," made waves on the radio. The album sold another million copies at the beginning of 1996, and the "Brain Stew" video, which included a tacked-on video for the hyperactive bonus track "Jaded," proved popular on MTV. "Walking Contradiction," the fourth and final single from *Insomniac*, finally reached the Billboard charts, peaking at number 5 on the Modern Rock chart. The video, featuring the band members strolling through a gritty neighborhood and causing a little mayhem, earned them a Grammy nomination (although they lost to the Beatles's "Free as a Bird" clip). In March of 1996, they won two Bay Area Music awards, for Best Hard Music Album and Outstanding Drummer, proving that not everyone back home despised them.

THE ROAD GETS ROUGHER

On tour, things didn't go as well for the band. They launched a world arena tour in early 1996, with old friends The Mr. T. Experience opening. Although the shows usually sold out thanks to their signature low prices, there was no denying the band had left Gilman Street far behind. Armstrong voiced his discomfort with constantly playing arenas, and the performances lost some of their explosive energy. The grind of constant travel got to all three of them. "On tour we have the most exciting lives in the world for one hour a day," Dirnt said, "and the rest of the time it's the most boring job in the world."[15] The fans, too, didn't get as involved in the shows. "When kids used to come to our shows, they used to come like a community, to hang out and be part of a punk atmosphere," Armstrong told *BAM* magazine, "Now it's more like 'Alright, motherf***** . . . entertain my f***** ass right now.'"[16]

Not only did the fans sometimes let them down, the band members also had to go without the support of their families. They dreaded leaving their wives and children behind. It was especially difficult to stay in touch in Europe, as this was long before cell phones were mainstream—they couldn't always find a usable phone to call home. "I'd rather be the station wagon kind of parent, you know, like going to Wally World," Armstrong said. "I just want to be a normal dad."[17] As someone whose father had died young, the thought of abandoning his kids for months at a time unsettled him.

He still didn't exactly match the common conception of a typical dad, as is clear in a series of letters he exchanged with an irate mother in late 1996. This mother had caught her eight-year-old son listening to a copy of *Insomniac* that his grandmother had bought for him (presumably the grandmother hadn't seen the "Geek Stink Breath" video). She called the record "trash" and ended with the outburst, "Why don't you do something positive and clean up your act? All the thought you are putting into the minds of our youth is scary." Armstrong shot back, "I don't make music for parents, grandparents or eight-year-olds and I'll say what I damn well please. That's the difference between you and me—I do what I want . . . you do what you're told. Obviously we're not on the same planet."[18] Rockers in the spotlight undoubtedly receive letters from angry parents pretty often, but Armstrong's decision to respond seems unusual. By this point, though, he was quick to defend himself against constant accusations from both sides: old fans accused Green Day of losing its edge, but at the same time the band was often seen as too hard-edged for their new younger fans.

The band's reactions to their own fans in the press revealed mixed feelings about their spreading popularity. In the same *Rolling*

Stone interview, Armstrong defends new listeners, and Dirnt seems angry at them. Armstrong asserts that he's grateful for the chance to play arenas on the *Insomniac* and *Dookie* tours, because it gave them a way to reach even more people. "I'm not going to sit here and say, 'F*** our fans, man, they're not true Green Day fans because they heard us on MTV.' These people are paying to see me play. A lot of those kids have never heard the kind of music that we play before, and a lot of them are from somewhere where there's a single parent that works their ass off to give them twelve bucks to go out and see us play this show."[19] He's able to take a populist view of things for a moment and appreciate the good in spreading punk rock where it might not otherwise reach.

Later in the interview, Mike takes a different tone, showing the strain of long tours and too much time spent in the public eye. He tells a story about meeting one fan on the run between the arena and the tour bus in England, who wanted to hang out with the band and wouldn't take no for an answer. "He's squeezing my hand really hard and saying, 'Why don't you give something back to your fans? I think you owe us.' . . . I looked at him and said, 'You know what? F*** you! You think that because you bought one record that you own me?'"[20] Putting yourself out there for the fans sounds like a great idea, but nobody can be accessible and community-minded all the time. Privacy is essential, especially for people who don't get much of it.

Dirnt's unease during this time surfaced in physical illnesses that sometimes hampered his performances. He told *Guitar World* that he was having panic attacks nearly every day. "Basically they wanted me on Xanax or Prozac all the time," he said. "And I wasn't going to do it. I'd only take Xanax when I got so nauseous I couldn't go on stage."[21] His heart problems, which had started a couple of years earlier, worsened. His heartbeat would speed up suddenly and leave him gasping, yet doctors couldn't tell what was causing it.

Armstrong kept a trick up his sleeve for rough nights: getting naked. "It usually happens when the shows are sort of mediocre," he said in a November 19 interview, "like when a show doesn't completely kick ass, you know? And the energy we're getting from the audience isn't too great, and the audience isn't getting good feedback from us. So I give them something to remember—even if it's not very big."[22] Two days after that article was published, Green Day played a mediocre show in Milwaukee to about 6,000 people. According to Armstrong, he dropped his pick and had to bend over to pick it up. According to Lieutenant Thomas Christopher of the Milwaukee

Police Department, "Mr. Armstrong dropped his pants to his knees and exposed his buttocks to the crowd."[23] Armstrong got dragged down to the station and received a citation for indecent exposure, then posted bail for $141.85 and skipped town.

After years of constant ups and downs, Green Day pulled the plug on their European tour in late 1996, claiming exhaustion. They were only a few months into another yearlong tour. "It was necessary for us just to go away at that point," said Cool. "It was a question of mental health on all three of our parts. We were in a bad state—not just with each other, but with the whole thing. So we just went away snowboarding for a while and forgot about the responsibility of being in a band, selling records and stuff."[24]

"The whole period wasn't a great time for us," Armstrong recalled years later. "We were doing stupid things, like trying to manage ourselves. And when we played live, we were playing way too fast—we had no groove, so that even the shows sounded as if we were trying to get the whole thing over with. And basically, something had to give."[25] This could have been the point at which Green Day burned out, like so many other bands that have rocketed to fame. Luckily, they had a home base to return to, and enough ambition to ensure this was really just a break, not a breakup.

NOTES

1. Lawrence Livermore, "*Hit List* Interview with Billie Joe," www.greenday .net/hitlistinterviewbj.html, July 18, 2001 (accessed January 10, 2009).
2. Craig Marks, "An American Family," *Spin*, December 1995, 58-61.
3. Marks, 138.
4. Jaan Uhelszki, "Pop Quiz: Q&A With Billie Joe Armstrong of Green Day," *San Francisco Chronicle*, Sunday, November 19, 1995, PK-44.
5. Alec Foege, "Green Day," *Rolling Stone*, December 28, 1995–January 11, 1996, 49.
6. Marks, 140.
7. Jaan Uhelszki, "It's Not Easy Being Green Day," *San Francisco Chronicle*, October 1, 1995, PK-31.
8. Marc Spitz, *Nobody Likes You: Inside the Turbulent Life, Times, and Music of Green Day* (New York: Hyperion, 2006), 120.
9. Marks, 140.
10. *Ibid.*
11. *Ibid.*
12. Doug Small, *Omnibus Press Presents the Story of: Green Day* (New York: Omnibus Press, 2005), 41.

13. Spitz, 124.
14. Uhelszki, "Pop Quiz: Q&A With Billie Joe Armstrong of Green Day," PK-44.
15. Foege, 50.
16. Spitz, 125.
17. Marks, 58.
18. Ben Myers, *Green Day: American Idiots and the New Punk Explosion* (New York: The Disinformation Company, Inc., 2006), 135.
19. Foege, 53.
20. Ibid.
21. Uhelszki, "Green Day Gets Bigwig Manager," *San Francisco Chronicle*, Sunday, July 28, 1996, PK-39.
22. Uhelszki, "Pop Quiz: Q&A With Billie Joe Armstrong of Green Day," PK-44.
23. Myers, 135.
24. Myers, 136.
25. Small, 43.

CHAPTER SIX

Out on a Limb

Green Day rallied during their time at home and began developing songs again, but this time they knew things had to change. They wouldn't sound credible if they just dropped another album full of pissed-off punk from their nice suburban neighborhoods. Armstrong's family had done a lot to give him a new perspective, and he was not about to pretend that everything was still the same. "Having a son has changed my ideas about life, and I reflect that in my writing," Armstrong said. "I am a father and I am a husband and I have this relationship with two people, but at the same time I want to be like an arrogant rock 'n' roll star. The two roles definitely clash."[1]

Tré Cool swore the two roles came together at a secret "welcome back" show they played on Valentine's Day in 1997, for just 150 friends. As he explained it, "We wanted to get them all hooked up! Boy met girl, girl met boy, boy met boy, and girl met girl. We like it when people fall in love at our shows. Also, when they get knocked up in the parking lot. As long as they bring the baby to the next tour and call it Nimrod, it's fine."[2] *Nimrod* would be the name of their next album, which attempted to bring together their newfound maturity and their own classic punk rock swagger.

Armstrong's ideas about music had changed along with his life. He, Cool, and Mike Dirnt knew that the next album had to be different and go further than the pop-infused punk of their past albums. The trio decided to stick with Rob Cavallo as producer, however, and do their experimenting within their trusted inner circle. To some extent, the story of the *Nimrod* era is the typical story of a famous band who gets bored with their old songs and more secure in their fame, and then decides to do their "experimental album" and indulge in rock-star excess. Often this story ends with a breakup or an overdose, but Green Day followed a more unexpected path.

THE TIME OF THEIR LIVES

They holed up in LA's Conway Studios, following such diverse artists as Michael Jackson, Linda Ronstadt, and the Offspring, and got ambitious together. The band had finished writing almost forty songs since they backed out of their European tour. The first departure: these songs hadn't been road-tested the way that most of the songs on previous albums had been. The second departure: the band had four months of recording, a previously unthinkable luxury.

With the help of several session musicians, including a full horn section, the band narrowed it down to eighteen songs, and almost as many musical styles. The songs dabbled in ska, rockabilly, surf, hardcore, and even string arrangements—by none other than Beck's father. Even the irrepressible Tré Cool got obsessive about recording. "Do you want to hear my trick?" he asked an interviewer. "When we were doing drum tracks, I had a Dr. Rhythm beat box and I'd set it on the tempo of the song we were going to record the next day. Then I'd put it in a drawer next to my head and just run it while I slept. It was totally this subliminal thing, and it worked great. When I'd get up to play the next day, I could lock onto that tempo and stay locked."[3] In the same interview, he went over all the drums he'd collected in the past few years (about twenty sets worth) and how each one could create a new sound. "They're all vintage drums, teched up just right, with the right head configurations, ready to record," he said.[4] Green Day was clearly ready to work hard on expanding their sound.

For the most part, they succeeded. The sing-along "Nice Guys Finish Last" would have fit on *Dookie* or even *Kerplunk!*, but "King for a Day" offered a wicked little take on current superstars and third wave ska pioneers, No Doubt, with horns and a bouncing bass line inspired by "Shout!" "Take Back" dove into classic hardcore for inspiration, and "Hitchin' a Ride" goes from a Middle Eastern string intro to a chugging chorus about falling off the wagon. An old song from before *Dookie* came back to life as "Haushinka," which alternates punk moments and nearly glam-metal moments. "We recorded it for [*Dookie*], but we didn't use it," said Cool. "And since then, we changed the arrangement and kind of rewrote the bass and drum parts, but still kept it the same song."[5]

The real high point of the album, though, is an even older song, the reflective ballad "Good Riddance (Time of Your Life)." It's an uncharacteristically sparse, mature song with not much else besides Armstrong's voice, acoustic guitar, and subtle strings. Armstrong had started an early version of the song around the time Green Day was recording their first album, but original drummer John Kiffmeyer rejected it for not being punk enough. The song took its current form during the *Dookie* sessions, but it still didn't seem to fit. Cavallo messed around with it for weeks before going into the studio to record *Nimrod*, trying to come up with an approach that would do it justice. "I was like, 'Oh my god, I know this song's a hit, but we just have to figure out how to do it. How do we do this song?' And when it came time for *Nimrod*, Billie said, 'I think this song will finally fit.' Then I said to myself, 'You know, the one thing that the song really needs is strings.' . . . They were definitely open to it, but it was a risk."[6] The band left the studio while Cavallo took about twenty minutes to record the whole string arrangement. "I knew it was a hit. And I was so excited, but I was all casual and I walked outside to the other building where they were playing foosball. The window was open and I looked in and said, 'Hey guys, you just cut a number one single.'"[7] Even though the song had undeniable pop appeal, Armstrong saw it as a real continuation of his punk rock roots. The emotion and vulnerability of the song made it more risky than some testosterone-fueled party anthem, and the departure from Green Day's past sound showed Armstrong's unwillingness to let his songwriting stagnate.

Meanwhile, although the recording sessions stayed productive, spending four months cooped up at the classic rock 'n' roll hotel, The Sunset Marquis, got to the band eventually, and the rock star attitude popped up again. Blame the boredom between sessions or even the LA smog—whatever it was, it went to their heads. Cool was the main source of ideas on how to shake up the monotony of hotel living. He got his hands on the hotel register one night after hearing that the Rolling Stones were in town. "I did it," he admitted. "I said to the desk clerk, 'You've got to make me another key, I've lost mine.'

And when he turned around I stole the register. And there was Keith Richards' phone number, so I called him in the middle of the night."[8] There was nudity in the halls, there was a near-fistfight with a 1980s pop star, there was a TV hoisted out a third floor window; what more could a rock star want? "There was a lot of glass," Armstrong recalled. "That's all I can tell you. You have to live that arrogant lifestyle every now and again."[9] Cool was even briefly rumored to be dating Winona Ryder, an actress with a notorious sweet tooth for rock boys.

Although the band officially denies it, the rumored apex of their antics came on Oscar night, when the actress Juliette Binoche was staying at the room directly below theirs. While she accepted her award for Best Supporting Actress in the highbrow drama, *The English Patient*, Dirnt accepted his inner child's advice and hung his rear end over the railing to deposit a special gift on her balcony. "She was so pissed she tried to get us thrown out of the hotel," Cool said. "But they let us stay. Big mistake.'"[10] Dirnt still swears it wasn't him.

They kept up the attitude into the summer before the album's release, booking a slot at Japan's Fuji Rock Festival alongside Foo Fighters, Beck, Prodigy, and the Red Hot Chili Peppers—all top names in mid-nineties rock. They played a secret show to warm up on July 19—not at a warehouse, but at Johnny Depp's club The Viper Room on LA's Sunset Strip. On the first day of the Fuji Rock Festival, Typhoon Rosie struck in the middle of the Red Hot Chili Peppers' set, trashing the grounds so badly that the whole festival was canceled and Green Day never got to play. The bands made up for it by heading to a local amusement park together. A drum-deprived Tré Cool can't be trusted, though: rumor has it that he started some high-jinks with the Foo Fighters drummer, Taylor Hawkins, in the middle of the park, and Armstrong had to defuse the situation with a joke. So Cool was spared yet another road injury.

Luckily, there were a couple of grownups behind the scenes by now. The band had stopped trying to manage themselves and promoted guitar tech and unofficial liason, Randy Steffes, to manager. Unfortunately, they just as quickly demoted him. "Randy isn't feeling too good right now," an insider confided to the *San Francisco Chronicle* at the time. "They told him they hired a new manager, and he took it pretty hard."[11] Steffes' replacement, Pat Magnarella of Atlas/Third Rail Management, had a good record as the manager of the Goo Goo Dolls, who broke big on the "alternative" scene in 1995, and the geek-chic band Weezer. Rob Cavallo's father, Bob, stood by as an unofficial management guru. (Steffes stuck by the band and eventually became the tour manager.) "It was just too much to deal with," Armstrong said after bringing Magnarella on board. "I wanna write songs. We didn't go around and whore ourselves to any other management. . . . We happened to luck out. There was no contract signed. It was pretty much a handshake and a nod and we had a manager."[12]

OUT TO THE FANS

With all the pieces in place, the first single was released three weeks ahead of the album on September 22, 1995. "Hitchin' a Ride" received heavy airplay and peaked at number five on the Billboard Modern Rock charts. Armstrong spoke to MTV news to preview the album's release, saying, "This record, more so than any other record, I think we sort of bled over this one a little more. I mean, this is a record I've been wanting to make since the band pretty much started."[13] The confident band members continued to stoke the interest in the album with a quick promotional tour of Europe, and landed back in New York for the October 14 album release party. They taped a Letterman appearance in the afternoon, and then gathered at the downtown club, Don Hill's, with a crowd of music industry insiders, drag queens, and Winona Ryder. The house band, Squeezebox, got things going, but late that night after the open bar had a chance to work its magic, Green Day took over to cover songs by Marilyn Manson, Cheap Trick, and The Who, as well as some old guilty pleasures like Def Leppard, Van Halen, and Survivor's "Eye of the Tiger." They tossed in a few of their own songs, and Tré closed with one of his own faux-country oddities.

The critics mostly stayed positive in the weeks following the release, although few people raved about the album. *Rolling Stone* awarded it three and a half stars, saying, "This music is a long way from Green Day's apprenticeship at the Gilman Street punk clubs, in Berkeley, Calif. But now that the band has seen the world, it's only fitting that Green Day should finally make an album that sounds as if it has."[14] *Billboard* noted that although Green Day songs don't automatically make listeners think of words like "growth" and "maturity," the terms were popping up in more and more discussions of this latest album. *Spin* and some other publications saw "growth" in a different light. "Anyone who ever griped that Green Day weren't really punk will find confirmation here," a reviewer said. "At heart, *Nimrod* is a poker-faced rendition of what every band before them has done in this situation—genre hopping, 'testing their boundaries' in the studio, strings, horns, the works."[15]

Armstrong stayed as confident as ever (and a little defensive, as ever) in the face of critics who thought *Nimrod* signaled that the band had left the last trappings of punk behind. "If there's such a thing as a stupid question," he said, "then that's it: 'Are you still punk?' I can't just shrug off my past, man."[16] He still considered himself a punk, still listened to punk, and still thought of his songs as punk, although his view of what that meant clearly differed from orthodox believers. For this album, he said, "We wanted to stretch as much as possible, but at the same time we never want to abandon the sound that we know how to do best."[17] The fans showed that they had come along for the ride as *Nimrod* went double platinum, just like *Insomniac* before it. Green Day had yet to repeat the huge success of *Dookie*, but they were holding their own.

To bring the fans in closer, Green Day nixed the arenas they had grown so sick of during the *Insomniac* tours and planned their fall 1997 tour around theaters that could accommodate one to three thousand fans. "The whole point of this tour is to be closer to the audience," Armstrong told reporters. "It's going to be just the three of us and them in smaller places. Dropping the front and being vulnerable is the main idea behind *Nimrod*."[18]

They certainly got up close and personal with the fans at their November in-store performance at Tower Records in New York. In between taping an appearance on *Late Night with Conan O'Brien* and playing a sold-out show at the Roseland Ballroom, the band members seized the opportunity to make a statement. With four hundred fans crowded among the CD racks and a thousand more peering through the plate-glass windows, Armstrong shouted from the top of the staircase, "Let's have a fucking riot!" During the eight-song set, Armstrong sprayed beer and water on the crowd (and the merchandise), dropped his pants for the benefit of the people outside, and spray painted "Nimrod" and "F*** you" on the window. A manager had to wrestle a 200-pound monitor out of his hands as he attempted to tip it over the staircase railing. After the last song, Cool tossed his bass drum from the second floor into the crowd below. "The store couldn't handle it," he laughed afterward.[19] Nobody got hurt, and nobody called the cops, but Tower had to shut down in order to clean up.

Many of the reports on the performance pointed out a certain contrived feeling to the anarchy, and wondered whether Green Day were just trying to prove they were still brats at heart, despite their serious attempt at growth in the studio. They may have just felt the pressure to live up to expectations: they were in the center of Manhattan, after all, doing a routine promotional appearance with members of the press watching. They could have quietly signed autographs and shaken hands with the store managers in order to sell more records, but their fans don't love them for their politeness and responsibility. Still, trashing a record store seemed a little obvious.

The next moment of chaos came just a week later, when the band played a free afternoon show in Toronto. An estimated 2,000-4,000 people (and several cops) crammed into a sixteen foot wide alley behind a record store for a glimpse of the band. Shows like this gave the band a better opportunity to do something unexpected without resorting to adolescent antics, working on the balance they had been trying to achieve since *Insomniac*'s release. "What I kind of came to is that it's OK to grow up, it's just slowing down that's the scary part," Armstrong said. "It's OK to grow up, but it doesn't mean you have to become like your parents."[20]

Nobody would have mistaken Green Day for ordinary parents at the December finale of their tour, K-ROQ's Almost Acoustic Christmas. They played the weekend festival in LA alongside David Bowie, No Doubt, Beck, Fiona Apple, Scott Weiland (on hiatus from Stone Temple Pilots), and punk upstarts Blink-182. Ever reluctant to disappoint a crowd, Armstrong mooned the audience and then threw a Christmas tree into the front row. It only got worse backstage. As Armstrong said, "After we played we found the button deal that makes the stage rotate. We were going to press it in the middle of the next band's set, but we got tackled by the stage hands. A bottle went through a window . . . Anyway, we got into someone's Bronco and left. My wife, Adrienne, was funny—she said, "Man, I never get to just hang out! I wanted to see Bowie!"[21] The police were called in because of the possible indecent exposure charges, but a K-ROQ spokeswoman explained to reporters that they would not press charges: "They played a really awesome set, and the audience just ate it up."[22]

Tré Cool did his share of rabble-rousing, trashing his kit almost every night on tour. It was right in line with his philosophy of mayhem. "Rock 'n' roll needs to come back around to the days of Keith Moon and The Who—just causing trouble, causing shit. That's our role now. We're the ones causing trouble, causing the most damage of any other band. And we have the power right now to do anything we want."[23]

They did use their powers for good sometimes. During this tour, the band established the well-loved tradition of pulling random audience members up on stage during a show to take over their instruments. They started by getting some lucky fan to take over the guitar at their European shows in 1997. "It really just involves the whole audience so much," said Bob Gruen, a well-known rock photographer who covered the tour. "I saw them one time where they had the kid literally jump out of the balcony and get caught by the crowd and passed up through the audience toward the stage."[24] The band started having a group of fans take over all their instruments to play the Operation Ivy song "Knowledge," which is both symbolic of Green Day's roots and easy to play. Those three chords built the kind of solid bond between the band and their fans that no amount of marketing can create.

GOOD RIDDANCE TO POP RUBBISH

Given the right song, though, marketing can create some unexpected bonds—between *Nimrod* and *Seinfeld*, between punk rock and proms. The single "Good Riddance" came out in January 1998, and something about the simple melody and heartfelt lyrics swept into every corner of pop culture. It translated into almost any context. Easy listening stations got hold of it, England's national soccer team played it when they lost at the World Cup, and the Chicago Bulls bid Michael Jordan farewell with it at his final game. The hospital drama *ER* used the song in a funeral scene for a young cancer patient. "I heard that it was going to be on," Armstrong shrugged, "but I kinda purposely didn't watch it because that show is too heavy for me and I don't like having my evening filled with people dying of f*****-up diseases."[25] Most famously, "Good Riddance" provided the soundtrack for the season finale of the groundbreaking sitcom, *Seinfeld,* in April 1998. It gave the highlight reel of memorable clips a feeling of reflection without sentimentality, which actually fit the song pretty well.

The video for "Good Riddance (Time of Your Life)" is one of the few quiet videos the band has ever made. The way it swoops in on people of all ages, all over the city, suggests that they knew how universal the message of transition and moving on could be. And, thanks to this song, after being nominated thirteen times before, Green Day finally won an MTV Video Music Award.

All this had a strange effect on the clan they'd left behind at 924 Gilman Street, even more confusing than when *Dookie* went platinum. "How ironic is it that Green Day songs are played at high school proms?" asked Mike K., a show coordinator at Gilman when

Green Day first formed. "Those of us that wanted to spread the punk message to the larger world got our wish, and now we're left dazed, wondering what the f*** happened."[26]

BACK TO BERKELEY

The same month that Green Day's departure from punk began to spread through mainstream culture, one of the pillars of the East Bay punk subculture took his leave. Tim Yohannan, the founder of *Maximumrocknroll* and 924 Gilman, died at home among friends at age 52, on April 3, 1998. He had suffered from non-Hodgkins lymphoma for some time.

Even though Green Day and Yohannan had disagreed from the beginning, with Yohannan rejecting Sweet Children's demos as "not punk enough," the band, like so many others, owed their early success to him and the community he had kept alive. He was instrumental in spreading the word about punk rock and connecting people across the globe through the *Maximumrocknroll* "scene reports" from different cities and countries. Before the Internet was more than a gleam in the government's eye, *MRR* readers were figuring out how to distribute foreign albums in their own countries and arguing over the meaning of punk rock in the letters section. The zine was arguably the first global self-created youth movement, former reader Gavin McNett wrote in an obituary: "For a teenage punk rocker in the '80s—a rare, thinly spread sort of demographic entity—to link up with punks in Sao Paulo, Bangkok and Greenland was a world-changing experience."[27]

Now Green Day was touring the far-flung cities they had once read about in the pages of *MRR*. They knew the value of the community that had started them down their path, and felt a need to reach out and participate once again. Armstrong and his wife, Adrienne, along with a group of friends, had hatched the idea of forming a record label in 1997, and now, at the moment when one important link in East Bay punk was severed, they created a new link by releasing their first album: One Man Army's LP, *Dead End Stories*.

The label, named Adeline Records after a Berkeley street, first got started around a firepit in an East Bay backyard. The Armstrongs and their friends, Jason White of Screw 32, Jim Thiebaud of Real Skateboards, and Lynn Parker, were talking about how fun it would be to release albums by bands they liked. Thiebaud couldn't stop thinking about working with One Man Army, and so the friends squeezed an office into someone's dining room and started working for free whenever they had spare time. "When we first started out we were doing everything ourselves," Adrienne Armstrong said. "We didn't know what we were doing."[28] They were determined not to coast to success on Green Day's fame, but it was all uphill at first. It took endless phone calls to get stores to stock their records, and the operation was too small to interest distribution companies. Thiebaud and Billie Joe printed T-shirts and patches by hand in the garage at first. Billie Joe's longtime side project, Pinhead Gunpowder, signed with the label early on, and the earliest signees, AFI and One Man Army, toured constantly, raising the label's profile nationwide.

Over the next few years, the label signed more bands and found official distribution, but the founders tried to keep it personal and pay attention to the bands working to make it to the next level. "We keep the demos in a big box," Adrienne explained. "Whenever Billie Joe comes home he digs through. He'll sit there for hours. Pop in one tape, listen, pop in the next one."[29] Adrienne played a large part in running the label (and does to this day), which was good, because her husband didn't have much spare time.

ROCK TILL YOU DROP

As Adeline Records was getting on its feet, Green Day embarked on the next big tour: they covered Europe from Ireland to Slovenia, then skipped over to Japan. They landed in Australia and New Zealand next, and caused something of a dust-up on Recovery TV in Australia during their live appearance on April 8, 1998. They were only there for an interview, but they decided to grab the house band's instruments anyway. They laid into an uncensored version of "The Grouch," and promptly got booted off the set. The misadventures continued back home: during a "secret" show for MTV's *Live From the Ten Spot* in San Francisco at Bottom of the Hill, Mike tossed in a stage jump that smashed his bass into his face, and he played the rest of the show with blood flowing from his nose. The American leg of the tour started April 30 in Houston—with a horn section. It was the first time Green Day had toured with more than the official trio. Joe McNally and Brodie Johnson of the Voodoo Glow Skulls played trumpet and trombone respectively until the May 9 show in Asbury Park, New Jersey, when No Doubt's trumpet player, Stephen Bradley, and trombonist, Gabe McNair, took over.

Mike, always accident-prone, got some help racking up his next injury during the LA radio station K-ROQ's annual Weenie Roast festival in June. Green Day played alongside alternative acts like Everclear, Deftones, Marcy Playground, and Third Eye Blind. While Green Day was on stage, Third Eye Blind bassist, Arion Salazar, ran out and bear-hugged Dirnt. Dirnt shook him off, and the scuffle turned into a fight before a Green Day roadie stepped in and Salazar was escorted offstage. After the show, Dirnt confronted Salazar backstage, and, while they were arguing, Dirnt was hit in the head with a beer bottle. K-ROQ initially reported that Salazar had hit him, but Third Eye Blind and onlookers blamed a fan who had just gotten Salazar's autograph. The bottle caused a fracture in Dirnt's skull, and he had to go to the hospital for twenty stitches and cancel the band's next show. Salazar apologized via press release: "I am sorry that my attempt at doing something I thought would be funny escalated into Mike getting hurt. That was never my intention. I simply had too much to drink and made a very bad decision. If I had been in Mike's place, I would have acted similarly. My heart goes out to him and I hope he recovers quickly. We have many friends in common and I just hope that he can accept my sincerest apology. I am sorry Mike."[30] In essence: "Please don't sue me!" Dirnt didn't file charges, although rumor has it that Green Day hired a private investigator to look into the incident.

Tensions ran high between the bands for months, and music publications seized on the "feud," but it ran its course within a year. Kevin Cadogan, Third Eye Blind's guitar player, read about an attack on a fifteen-year-old boy from Alameda who had been stabbed with a screwdriver by another boy. He arranged to meet the boy and give him a vintage guitar signed by all the band members. On his way to the hospital, he saw Mike Dirnt walk into a flower shop. "I was a little nervous," said Cadogan," but I figured he was not gonna try to kick my ass in a flower shop. So I went in and said hello. . . . It was a very un-rock 'n' roll moment. We talked about the incident in LA and agreed it was stupid and we should put it behind us." When Dirnt heard where Cadogan was going, he bought a card right then for Cadogan to take with him. "He wrote this nice message," Cadogan recalled. "He said something like, we all take a beating sometimes; it's how we get up that makes the difference."[31]

The band may have matured in many ways, but in others they remained very much the same. All the rock star antics took their toll, as the band started to slip a little. Their next single, "Redundant," peaked at number sixteen on the charts, the lowest of all the *Nimrod* singles. The album had hit double platinum, roughly the same level as *Insomniac*, but critics speculated that their audience would only keep diminishing. Armstrong had gained some weight from drinking endless beers in endless dressing rooms before shows, and later called this his "fat Elvis period." "I kind of became everybody's weird uncle," he said in 2004. "I was just drunk all the time and wearing a f****** leopard G-string. What's not to love about that? So I cut back on drinking beer. I had no balance in my life—I had to start taking better care of myself."[32]

There was no time for balance right away, though, as the endless *Nimrod* tour rolled on. The band turned down the Lollapalooza festival that year, as did Foo Fighters, Marilyn Manson, and Garbage, and the granddaddy of the alternative music festivals pulled the plug on itself. Green Day's U.S. tour ended in Seattle on August 1, 1998, at the radio station KNDD's Endfest, where, instead of taking a bow, they lit Cool's drum kit on fire. They left the country after that for the August festival season in Europe. After the Pukkelpop Festival in Belgium on August 30, they called it quits and hurried home—Armstrong's second son, Jakob Danger, was born on September 12.

After taking less than a month to bond with his new son, Armstrong and the band ran down to South America, playing seven shows in Argentina, Brazil, and Chile in November. They also found time to shoot the video for the last single from *Nimrod*, "Nice Guys Finish Last" and squeeze in a little more controversy. The College of the Canyons in Santa Clara, California, had agreed to host the football scene, but K-ROQ leaked the news and college officials cancelled the shoot, worried that their campus would be taken over by fans. K-ROQ announced the cancellation, and the college immediately reversed their decision and allowed the show to go on.

Green Day rang in 1999 at MTV's Times Square studios, playing the New Year's Eve show alongside rap metal act Limp Bizkit, R&B queen Aaliyah, and rapper Method Man of the Wu-Tang Clan. After all that, they decided they deserved a break. Only days after they announced that they would be supporting the Rolling Stones for five dates on their *No Security* tour, the band backed out without an official explanation. "I think we were pretty burned coming off tour," Armstrong said in late 2000. "I spent so much time away from my kids. My wife was having a baby. I was sort of a wreck, and I really needed to get back in the swing of my family life and my kids and my personal life. You have to have your own life, and you have to explore things on your own to be able to write good songs that people can relate to. I just don't want to be one of those guys singing about the next hotel room."[33] Once again, Green Day had toured till they dropped, and needed some serious time off to recharge. And once again, the next album would prove that they had plenty of new things to say.

NOTES

1. Jaan Uhelszki, "Green Day: Still a Bunch of Punks," *San Francisco Chronicle*, Sunday, October 12, 1997, PK-45.
2. Ben Myers, *Green Day: American Idiots and the New Punk Explosion* (New York: The Disinformation Company, Inc. 2006), 141.
3. Matt Peiken, "Green Day's Tré Cool: Hungry for Drumming," *Modern Drummer*, May 1998, 52.
4. *Ibid.*, 50.
5. *Ibid.*, 51.
6. Marc Spitz, *Nobody Likes You: Inside the Turbulent Life, Times, and Music of Green Day* (New York: Hyperion, 2006), 131.
7. Ibid., 131-132.
8. Uhelszki, PK-45.
9. *Ibid.*
10. Ibid.
11. Uhelszki, "Green Day Gets Bigwig Manager," *San Francisco Chronicle*, Sunday, July 28, 1996, PK-39.
12. Spitz, 129.
13. Doug Small, *Omnibus Press Presents the Story of: Green Day* (New York: Omnibus Press, 2005), 46.
14. Ibid.
15. Spitz, 133.
16. Myers, 147.
17. Uhelszki, PK-45.
18. Small, 48.
19. Myers, 149.
20. Lawrence Livermore, "*Hit List* Interview with Billie Joe," www.green-day.net/hitlistinterviewbj.html, July 18, 2001 (accessed January 10, 2009).
21. Jane Ganahl, "Has Billie Joe Grown Up?" The San Francisco *Examiner*, Sunday, December 14, 1997, section D.
22. Ganahl, section D.
23. Peiken, 46.
24. Spitz, 136.
25. Myers, 152.

26. Brian Edge, *924 Gilman: The Story So Far* (San Francisco: Maximumrocknroll, 2004), 107.

27. Gavin McNett, "The Day Punk Died: Tim Yohannon: 1946–1998," Salon.com, April 3, 1998, http://archive.salon.com/music/feature/1998/04/17feature.html (accessed February 16, 2009).

28. Fred Medick, "Sweet Adeline: A determinedly small Oakland label proves that punk is still a viable sound," *SF Weekly*, October 04, 2000, 1, http://www.sfweekly.com/2000-10-04/music/sweet-adeline/ (accessed February 16, 2009).

29. Medick, 2.

30. MTV News, "Green Day/Third Eye Blind Skirmish Results In Skull Fracture, Canceled Concerts," MTV.com, June 22, 1998, http://www.mtv.com/news/articles/1429740/19980622/green_day.jhtml (accessed February 19, 2009).

31. Jane Ganahl, "Boy's plight unites rival rock bands," The San Francisco *Examiner*, Friday, May 14, 1999, section C.

32. Caryn Ganz, "Intimate Portrait: Billie Joe Armstrong," *Spin* magazine, September 10, 2004, http://spin.com/articles/intimate-portrait-billie-joe-armstrong (accessed March 20, 2009).

33. Small, 59.

Never-before-published photo of Billie Joe Armstrong, age 18, playing at 924 Gilman Street on Aug. 31, 1990. This was the year after Sweet Children officially changed their name to Green Day and just a few months after Lookout! Records released the band's first LP, 39/Smooth. (Murray Bowles)

Never-before-published photo of Mike Dirnt and Tré Cool, both age 18, at Ugene's in the Bay Area on Jan. 26, 1991. Cool had only started playing with Green Day in November 1990. The band hadn't even gone on tour together yet, but they already knew they were on to something. (Murray Bowles)

Billie Joe Armstrong on stage at Woodstock '94, Aug. 14, 1994, in Saugerties, New York. His clothes are clean, which means the rush of mudslinging that made this performance so memorable hasn't started yet. (AP Photo/Robert F. Bukat)

Mike Dirnt, Tré Cool, and Billie Joe Armstrong of Green Day celebrate their best alternative music video award, for "Time of Your Life," at the MTV Video Music Awards in Los Angeles, Sept. 10, 1998. (AP Photo/Michael Caulfield)

Never-before-published photo of Billie Joe Armstrong at the Warped Tour in 2000, just before the release of Warning. *During a slow period in their career, the band scaled back from arena shows to the smaller punk rock Warped Tour to remind their core fans how electric a Green Day show could be. (Edwina Hay)*

Billie Joe Armstrong performs "American Idiot" with Green Day at the 47th Annual Grammy Awards on Sunday, Feb. 13, 2005, in Los Angeles. The band was nominated for six awards and took home the Grammy for Best Rock Album. American Idiot *was the breakout hit of the year, topping the charts in the United States, the UK, Australia, Canada, and Japan. (AP Photo/Kevork Djansezian)*

Billie Joe Armstrong performs with Green Day at the Live 8 concert in Berlin, July 2, 2005. The 10 simultaneous concerts held that day were aimed at pressuring world leaders to drop the debt of developing nations and increase aid to Africa—and it worked. (AP Photo/Jan Bauer)

Green Day poses on the white carpet of the MTV Video Music Awards Aug. 28, 2005, in Miami. They took home seven awards, including Video of the Year for "Boulevard of Broken Dreams." (AP Photo/Jeff Christensen)

Mike Dirnt on stage at Giants Stadium in East Rutherford, New Jersey, Sept. 1, 2005. The band wasted no time in getting back on tour after their seven wins at the MTV Video Music Awards. (AP Photo/Rich Schultz)

Tré Cool performs in Foxboro, Massachusetts, Sept. 3, 2005. The American Idiot *tour lasted well over a year, making it the longest outing of the band's career. (AP Photo/Robert E. Klein)*

Tré Cool, left, Billie Joe Armstrong, center, and Mike Dirnt arrive on stage to accept the Grammy for record of the year for "Boulevard of Broken Dreams," a single from American Idiot, *at the 48th Annual Grammy Awards on Feb. 8, 2006, in Los Angeles. The band recovered their friendship as well as their careers during their intensive work on the album. (AP Photo/Mark J. Terrill)*

Mike Dirnt, left, Billie Joe Armstrong, center, and Tré Cool goof off back-stage, holding their Grammies for record of the year for "Boulevard of Broken Dreams," on Feb. 8, 2006. (AP Photo/Reed Saxon)

From left, Mike Dirnt, Billie Joe Armstrong, and Tré Cool of Green Day pose at the Mercer Hotel in New York, on May 15, 2009, the same day their new album 21st Century Breakdown *was released. The album hit number 1 on the Billboard charts the first week. (AP Photo/Bruce Gilbert)*

CHAPTER SEVEN

Early Warning

As soon as anyone loses momentum in the pop culture rat race, the next competitor is right there waiting to take their place. Green Day laid low for most of 1999, and while they were out, Blink-182 released their homage to *Dookie, Enema of the State*. With scatological humor, loud guitars, and vocal harmonies, they won over the fans who were a little too young to remember Green Day's arena-rocking heyday. Blink-182 and the other pop punk bands who rose to popularity around this time paid a lot of respect to Green Day, even while outselling them. By 1999, Green Day was hanging in a kind of limbo: their Gilman fans were turning thirty, and the younger fans brought on board by *Dookie* were in college and outgrowing them. Punk had given way briefly to ska, and now rap metal was the reigning sound. Kids who might have found their way to Green Day started turning to the younger pop punk bands.

Green Day themselves had changed, though, slowly continuing to figure out their own way of growing up. The millennium found them at a crossroads with the potential to leave their manic days behind them. "I spend all my time at home parenting," Billie Joe Armstrong said. "I have no kind of rock star lifestyle whatsoever. Call it a curse, call it a blessing. But when I'm at home, I'm Daddy. I rarely go out. I get up at six a.m. I do a little lawn-mowing now and again.

I don't think I really do anything my broke friends can't do."[1] Well, at least Armstrong hadn't lost his defensive anti-rock-star streak. And Mike Dirnt may have taken up golf, but he wasn't exactly traditional about it. "I played a little bit of golf," he said. "Do you know why? Because a bunch of my friends said, 'Dude, c'mon, man, we drink as much as we can!' You've gotta picture this, there's all these guys in leather jackets digging holes in the course and pissing off all the other golfers."[2]

Dirnt stayed active musically with his side project, the Frustrators, with Terry Linehan from Waterdog and Jason Chandler and Art Tedeschi from Violent Anal Death. They recorded their album *Bored in the USA* in 1999, and they released it on Adeline in 2000. When they tried out their songs at 924 Gilman Street, Dirnt didn't get booed offstage or protested outside the venue. They released a second album, *Achtung Jackass*, in 2002. Armstrong kept his hand in by producing two records for Adeline, *Last Word Spoken* by the label's first signees, One Man Army, and *Burning Flesh and Broken Fingers* by the Criminals. He also kept writing songs, and in November of 1999 the band debuted the song "Warning" at one of their rare shows. They played the Bridge School Benefit at the Shoreline Amphitheater in Mountain View, California, an annual benefit for handicapped children's education founded by Neil Young.

COMING AROUND AGAIN

The show and the new songs taking shape jolted the band back into action, and they began making plans to record an album titled *Warning*, after the song. They had reached a crossroads in their lives as they neared thirty; they knew punk had come and gone from the mainstream, and they were also ready to move toward something new. The first step down this new road was choosing a new producer. Rob Cavallo stepped back and Scott Litt, with credits including Nirvana, R.E.M., and the Replacements, stepped in. "I'm excited about it," Litt told *Rolling Stone* in January of 2000. "Some of the songs I've heard are really special."[3] Green Day next announced that they would play Warped Tour that summer.

Their plans hit a snag soon after they started recording, though, and by mid-February Litt was out. "It just didn't work out," Armstrong told *Alternative Press* in a rare comment on the split. "He was really cool, but for that particular project, it just wasn't the right chemistry."[4] Cavallo came back, although only as an executive producer, and Green Day handled the main producer duties themselves.

Armstrong prepped for recording by pulling out an old Bob Dylan album, *Bringing It All Back Home*. The 1964 classic saw the folk star working with a band for the first time, with half the songs going in an acoustic protest-song direction, and half aiming for experimental electric blues. Not the most typical influence on a punk songwriter, but Green Day wanted some fresh ideas. They had already proved they wouldn't be pigeonholed into one sound, and wanted to take it even further this time.

They took it a little too far on "Blood, Sex, Booze"—at least their sound engineer might have thought so. The engineer, Tone, was only twenty, and Tré thought it would be funny to get him to spice up the beginning of the song. He called up a local dominatrix named Mistress Simone and brought her in to teach Tone a lesson. "It was f******* cool," laughed Tré. "She was kicking him in the nuts, stamping on his nipples with big ol' f******* heels. He was scared but now he's into it!"[5]

Not all the songs had that kind of intensity, though: the band kept going for variety, and refused to put pressure on their creativity. "Billie really waited for inspired moments, especially lyrically inspired moments," recalled Dirnt. "And you know, we weren't forcing songs. When we'd have two, three songs, we'd start another one and we'd go, 'Uh, that's not working today. Let's go work on the ones that do work.' Whereas on the last record, we were just pounding songs out, as many as we could."[6] This thoughtful approach showed through in the mellower acoustic sound they developed on many songs, complete with harmonicas. They weren't just doing what was expected of them, or what they thought people expected them to do, and it took some of the weight off them. "Hold On" echoed Beatles pop and Dylan folk, while "Macy's Day Parade" brought an acoustic touch to lyrics about the emptiness of commercialism. Dirnt explained "Warning" as a song about "being surrounded by outside information, about warning labels and signs that direct you where to go in life, but are really just representative of this general false sense of freedom that America seems to exploit all the time, probably now more so than ever."[7] "Waiting" embraced pure pop, with a chorus modeled on Petula Clark's 1964 hit "Downtown," and offered a sunny view of doing your best in uncertain times. Armstrong cited the song as one that he'd want his sons to be influenced by and explained that it was "about putting your best foot forward, even if you don't have any idea what's in store for the future, about trying to make a difference in your own life, about having high goals even though you're not fully sure of what you want or where you're going to end up."[8] On a similar note, "Minority" went back to the punk principle of thinking for yourself regardless of what anyone else is doing.

THE SHAPE OF THINGS TO COME

"There's a sense of hope in this record, on a personal level and for humanity in general," Armstrong said after recording. "I don't think there is anything on here that is too self-absorbed or dwells on the negative."[9] In taking this broader view with lyrics that were less dark, not to mention throwing in the acoustic guitar, Green Day put themselves far outside the mainstream, where the harsher sounds of nu-metal bands like Limp Bizkit and Korn ruled radio. As in the song, Armstrong relished being in the "Minority." While acknowledging that angst can be constructive, as in Fugazi's music, he questioned bands like Korn and Marilyn Manson. "There are a lot of angsty metal bands around right now, but I want to know what they are angry about and what they're going to do to make it better. If it's angst that's being used for showmanship then I can't take them seriously because there's no sort of intellect being applied, it's just testosterone."[10]

Part of the heightened awareness in *Warning* came out of the band members' increasing attention to politics and the state of the country as a whole, rather than just the punk community or the Bay Area. They were recording in an election year, with Democratic President Bill Clinton leaving office after two terms. Clinton's vice-president, Al Gore, faced off against George W. Bush, a Republican and the son of former President George H. W. Bush. The leftist consumer-rights activist Ralph Nader made a stand as the candidate of the upstart Green Party, offering a true alternative, however hopeless it was that he would actually succeed. The campaign was well underway by late spring, when recording wrapped up. "It didn't look good for Al Gore," Armstrong said. "It was just sort of a feeling that I knew there was going to be someone really conservative who was going to come into office. And after [Bush] was elected, we watched the culture sort of sway. And that's one reason why I was really taking my time writing songs to really [make an impact]. Instead of just writing an overly knee-jerk reaction."[11] Although the album didn't come out in time to be thought of as a protest or an endorsement of one candidate's views, it supports the kind of independent thought and questioning that are so important when decision time comes around.

Armstrong saw politics as more than just the American two-party system, and brought it down to the way people choose to live their lives. "There's a lot of people that [didn't] vote this year just because of lack of a better selection," he said after the election, "The way I look at it, every dollar I spend is a vote. Where are you going to put your dollar? What is worth investing into? Is it gonna be the Starbucks in town, or is it gonna be your local coffee place, or small business people that are just trying to put food on the table?"[12]

THE SUMMER CAMPAIGN

The band later took their disillusionment with the 2000 election and put it to good use, but as the year moved on and the election drew closer, they concentrated on getting the message of *Warning* out. In the time between wrapping up recording and releasing the album, they hooked up with the Warped Tour for the summer. Before they left, Cool, who had divorced Lisea a while back (the band has always been vague on the date), married his fiancée, Claudia, in May. After a quick honeymoon, the band got rolling again.

Even though the Warped Tour wasn't exactly ideologically pure, given its many corporate sponsorships and the association with extreme sports, it was a step back for the band and a chance to reconnect with more underground punk bands like NOFX and the Donnas. Although Green Day was clearly the main draw, Warped made a point of not identifying any one artist as the headliner. It seemed a little strange for Green Day to be playing at this level, as a band who had filled stadiums just a few years back. "They were the biggest band on that tour but it wasn't by far," recalls Fat Mike of NOFX. "Green Day weren't super popular at that time. I think they did the Warped Tour because they *wanted* to get popular again. There's very few bands that can have a long career at such a high level."[13] Green Day may have realized that if they couldn't carry arenas on their own at this point, they should work on rebuilding their grassroots community.

Tré Cool didn't mind telling it like it was. "We've got to stake our claim a little bit, to remind everybody who's the best," he told MTV. "We haven't played live for a while, and I think people are forgetting. There's a lot of imitators out there, so we've got to remind people. . . .

They remember, but if they can't get Pepsi, they're going to get RC, you know. They can't get the real, they're going to get the substitute."[14] Though they didn't test out any new material, they did add one more war wound to the list: Cool sacrificed part of a toe after his cymbals went flying. The band played thirty-nine shows in forty-four days, doing all they could to remind their core fans of the songs they loved and get them excited for more.

The pressure was on, and not just because of the upcoming album. The Recording Industry Association of America, which certifies sales of gold and platinum records (500,000 copies and 1,000,000 copies), had just added the Diamond category, for albums selling at least 10,000,000 copies. *Dookie* was up there in this new category, along with Michael Jackson, the Eagles, Madonna, and Beatles. It was just one more reminder of the heights they had reached in the past.

Starting with the Warped Tour, they made one important break with tradition: they brought a second guitarist, Jason White, on board to beef up their live shows. White showed up in the East Bay in 1992, fresh from Little Rock, Arkansas, attracted by the active punk scene. After a brief return to Arkansas in 1996, he settled permanently and joined Pinhead Gunpowder. He also helped launch Adeline and formed the Influents, who soon signed to the label. As a fellow Replacements fan, he picked up on Green Day's pop-influenced sound as soon as they asked him to join their live shows.

He came along for the ride to the UK in September, where the band played a few warm-up shows before the album's release. They appeared on the legendary BBC show *Top of the Pops* on the 14th, following in the footsteps of Jimi Hendrix, the Smiths, and Radiohead (not to mention Paula Abdul and Billy Ray Cyrus). The next day, they played a secret show in London at the King's College student union building to preview the new album and take requests from the crowd. Only 500 people were invited, but the show was broadcast on BBC Radio 1. Nearly all the reviews gushed about the band's powerful appeal and stage presence. "It was the best show we've ever played in the UK," Armstrong said later that week. "Doing interviews gets really monotonous—I think people can find out more about us and our individual characters by coming to see us live than sitting talking to us. Our music really needs to be seen live to be understood."[15]

The next day, they met up for a magazine photo shoot and discussed the after-hours action the night before. "Some girl invited me to a sex and drugs party at her flat," Cool recalled fuzzily. "She said she figured I was someone important because I was the only person in the club wearing shorts. And because I was American."[16] He declined the invitation. Dirnt had gone home early so he could get up and go shopping for used records in the morning, and showed up to the photo shoot bragging about the fifty-five rare seven-inch singles he'd just picked up cheap. After the magazine shoot, they filmed another TV appearance, and then played a late-night in-store show at the Virgin Megastore. The "Minority" single was released as soon as the clock struck midnight—but not before the band had trashed their gear and tagged "Green Day" and "Goodnight" on the walls.

WARNING SIGNS

That first single topped the Billboard Modern Rock chart in the U.S., but didn't crack the Hot 100. On October 3, 2000, *Minority* hit stores, with a special vinyl release handled by Adeline Records. (Vinyl was starting to make a comeback with collectors like Dirnt, and Adeline has continued to release a vinyl edition of each of Green Day's albums ever since.) In a disappointing turn of events, the album peaked at #4 on the Billboard Top 200 and quickly dropped out of sight. Reviews were mixed, as critics alternately saw Green Day shrinking back from their aggressive punk roots or sticking too closely to their established formulas. The songs didn't go over particularly well on radio, either, when stacked up against the likes of Limp Bizkit and Korn. "During that period, that was like late '90s, early 2000, they were kind of seen as elder statesmen," said Kevin Weatherly, program director of LA's adventurous station K-ROQ. "You had the whole rap-rock thing. And there was a period of time where we had a tough time getting that whole sound—it has nothing to do with Green Day—that sound we had a difficult time getting to work for us."[17]

Just to complicate things, an unknown, unsigned British band called the Other Garden threatened to sue Green Day, claiming that the song "Warning" plagiarized their 1997 song "Never Got the Chance." They contacted Green Day's labels in the United States and the UK with a request to freeze royalty payments, and Green Day issued a press release in their own defense. "Green Day denies the apparent accusations. If the claimants carry out their threats to sue Green Day, you can be sure that such a lawsuit will be defended vigorously."[18] The Brits later dropped the whole thing, but it was another irritation at an awkward moment for the band.

The band found themselves more reluctant to tour this time around. ""We really don't know what our touring is going to be like," Armstrong told *Rolling Stone* right after the album's release. "Adrienne and me were sitting here talking and we were like, 'We're *adults*.' I have to be home. I have a two-year-old and a five-year-old, and when I leave things fall apart. It's just too much for one person to handle. But I don't hate touring though—I love touring."[19] They started small, playing a string of radio station–sponsored shows in clubs instead of theaters and playing covers and audience requests rather than pushing all their new songs.

POLITICS AS USUAL

On November 5, with the Presidential election just two days away, Green Day took the opportunity to make a political statement of their own. They played in front of City Hall at the Take Back San Francisco protest, where musicians and artist demonstrated against the skyrocketing rents of the dot-com business boom and the city's ineffective support for the arts. As dot-com businesses sucked up money from investors, they poured it back into hip real estate in the city, and warehouse spaces and lofts that once provided cheap space for artists to live and work filled up with computers instead. Evictions became common, and club after club shut down. Downtown Rehearsal, a building used by about 500 bands, was sold in August 2000 and closed soon after to make room for more dot-coms. This massive loss catalyzed the community reaction, which included Take Back San Francisco and a "Million Band March" that started in the Mission and wound its way to City Hall in time for Green Day's show.

Resentment had been building in all corners of the local music scene, including studios. "In this marketplace, one can't make money in the studio business," said Dan Alexander, owner of Coast Recorders, founded in 1972. "It's just not happening. In my own particular case, my billionaire landlord took advantage of the fact that I was three days late on my rent to evict me."[20] John Lucasey, owner of Studio 880 in the East Bay, where Green Day had just recorded *Warning*, couldn't rest easy despite his facility's high profile. "San Francisco is not at 90%—it's at 120% capacity," he said of the struggle for real estate. "Everything is flooding over here, and there are a lot of unbelievably expensive high-tech lofts and buildings going up in our area. And labels are very watchful over their budgets. Unfortunately, a lot of bands just can't afford to stay in the Bay Area."[21] Green Day may have had the money to stay put, but they recognized the struggles of underground bands, and did what they could to help out.

Unfortunately, the pro-business, anti-art climate was not about to change, even as most of the dot-com companies ran out of steam in the next couple of years. After a highly contested election on November 7, 2000, and the recounts that went on for weeks afterward in Florida, the Republican George W. Bush was declared the new President of the United States of America. As Tré Cool put it, "I knew the day George Bush was elected president that we were in deep, deep shit."

Armstrong felt conflicted when faced with two candidates he saw as puppets of a political system that didn't offer a real choice. "I voted for [Ralph] Nader this time. I was sort of torn between that and the lesser of two evils argument. I don't know. I got there and I was going to vote for Gore, and as soon as I got inside the booth, I couldn't do it, so . . ." Nader, the Green Party candidate, seemed to offer an idealistic alternative to the traditional Republican/Democratic party standoff, but ended up with less than 3% of the vote. If the conservative victory did any good, though, it was in awakening a spirit of constructive rebellion in American youth and artists. "We all joked about when Bush got elected, how it's gonna make punk rock good for four years,"[22] laughed Fat Mike of NOFX. Soon enough, Green Day would find a way to express their disillusionment clearly and powerfully through their music.

For now, though, the band focused on the task at hand, playing shows in Europe and the United States before finishing up with another appearance at K-ROQ's Almost Acoustic Christmas. The single for "Warning" came out that December, with a video featuring a character ignoring the countless warnings society tries to put in his way: pulling the "Do Not Remove" tag off his mattress, drinking spoiled milk, crossing a police line, etc.

In January, the touring began in earnest: they played fifteen U.S. dates with the Get Up Kids, then jetted off to Japan. That June saw them loading into major arenas every night with Australian openers the Living End. Two months later, when they finally wrapped up the frenetic mix of requests, covers, fan participation, confetti cannons, and Armstrong's leopard-print thong, they took a deep breath and plunged right into Europe's late-summer festival season. They hit the legendary Reading and Leeds festivals on back-to-back days. "It is great when you can see an ocean of people in front of you," Armstrong recalled later. "I remember at Reading we played before Travis, and someone said, 'How are Travis going to follow that?' I like how they used the word 'that.' I like the fact that people describe our live show by asking the question, 'How is someone going to follow *that?*'"[23]

In between dates, Armstrong found time to co-write the song "Unforgiven" for a new album by the Go-Gos. The California new wave/punk band made history during the late 1970s and 1980s as the first all-woman band to play their own instruments and write their own songs to top the Billboard album charts. They reunited in 1999, and "Unforgiven" appeared on their critically acclaimed 2001 album, *God Bless the Go-Gos*. Their pop-influenced punk sound was a perfect fit for Armstrong's songwriting style. "[Green Day were] influenced by us, and we ended up getting re-influenced by them," guitarist Jane Wiedlin told MTV.[24]

DARKNESS COMING DOWN

Easter Sunday, 2001, cast a shadow over Green Day's accomplishments: the punk icon and their personal hero, Joey Ramone, died of lymphatic cancer at the age of 49. His fellow musicians poured out tributes to the influential singer and songwriter, including Joe Strummer of the Clash, Belinda Carlisle of the Go-Gos, Bono of U2, and members of Green Day. "Thanks always comes a day late and a dollar short," said Dirnt, "but my respect has and will always be there for the band that showed me that simple songs and a simple life could make you happy."[25] Armstrong summed it all up: "I can firmly say that rock 'n' roll will not be the same without Joey Ramone alive."

This was the first of a series of sad events for the year: the next came in June, when Dirnt's mother died of an illness related to alcohol abuse. Dirnt cited her death as one reason the band later refused to do beer advertisements.

Then came September of 2001. The terrorist attacks on the World Trade Center in New York and the Pentagon in Washington, D.C. erased any lingering euphoria from the summer tour for the band and their fans. "I was on West Coast time, so it was really early in the morning for me," Armstrong told *Kerrang!* at the end of 2001. "I saw the towers fall, and it felt like the world was gonna end."[26] As the United States marshaled the forces of war to bomb the Al Qaeda organization's camps in Afghanistan, the band spoke out against the fighting. "I object to any killing at all," Cool said. "You know it's terrible what happened and I think retaliation definitely makes sense and it's definitely one option. But, personally, I prefer peace. You know, maybe I'm just being ignorant and shortsighted, but I just don't think that killing people is a good way to remedy people dying. Martin Luther King Jr. said that you can murder a murderer but you can never murder murder itself."[27] The band did express dissent in their interviews and place an anti-war petition on their website—but in the face of so much upheaval, they, like many citizens, held their breath to see how the national response would play out. "I think after September 11, I took a step back," Armstrong recalled three years later. "As an artist, you get kinda like hesitant, thinking, 'I don't want to speak too soon. I know something's going to come out of this, but right now I have to process things because it just seems so unreal."[28] In the months following the terrorist attacks, the shift toward heavy-handed patriotism and unquestioning support of the government made an indelible impression on the band.

Maybe it was the vague sense of punk unity in the face of extreme conservatism, or the fact that personal disagreements suddenly seemed petty, but five days after the attacks, Green Day played their first show at 924 Gilman Street in eight years. During an Adeline Records showcase, the band members borrowed instruments from the other bands and took requests. With that, they closed out a full year of touring.

TAKING STOCK

With the *Warning* tour machine shut down for the winter and the peak sales for the album established as Green Day's lowest yet, the band members pulled back a bit. Rather than going into song-writing mode as they had after the tours for their previous albums, they followed up with a backward look at their career so far: the greatest-hits collection, *International Superhits*, released November 13, 2001. Reprise released a special edition of 4,000 records in pink and purple vinyl at the same time. The album covered only songs recorded for Warner Bros., so "Welcome to Paradise" and other equally worthy Lookout! songs didn't make the cut. Two new songs did, though: "Maria" and "Poprocks and Coke." The band made new videos for both songs for the companion DVD, *International Super-videos*. "Seeing a decade of your songs laid out like that is an invitation to a midlife crisis,"[29] Armstrong reflected later. The critics did start wondering aloud if this meant that no new material was forth-coming, that this signaled the end of the road for the band. But of course, the band's whole career had been on fast-forward—after all, Armstrong, Dirnt, and Cool were all still in their twenties.

The band laid low for the first chunk of 2002, but popped up at the Rock Hall of Fame's induction ceremony for the Ramones, pay-ing tribute to their heroes with a short, aggressive set: "Rockaway Beach," "Teenage Lobotomy," and "Blitzkrieg Bop." It was natural for the band to consider its legacy at this point, with their idols enshrined in the Hall of Fame and their own greatest hits all lined up in one album. If that wasn't enough, Dirnt underwent carpal tunnel surgery to repair the ravages of ten-plus years of bass, and Armstrong turned thirty on February 17.

At thirty, it doesn't look so good if you're only talking about pot and masturbation, but Green Day wasn't quite ready to let go of the past. That April, they teamed up with the scatological pop-punk act Blink-182 for the Pop Disaster Tour. Billed as a "shared bill," they took turns headlining and opening. Despite Blink-182's boy band–level record sales, it was a little blasphemous to see them take precedence over Green Day. Blink-182 applauded Green Day with-out going into how directly the older band had influenced them. "One of the first times I ever played music with Tom we were play-ing Green Day covers in his garage," Mark Hoppus said. "We have loved Green Day music since we started this band and they really opened a lot of doors and they kind of blazed a trail for our style of music, for sure."[30]

Green Day wasn't ready to let anybody talk down to them or write them off as a purely nineties band, though. They had always wanted to stick it out and grow, like the Ramones, the Clash, and the other time-less bands they admired. "They knew that if you said, 'Hey, punk band!' they were not necessarily the first group you thought of anymore," said their longtime producer Rob Cavallo. "But meanwhile, they knew they'd started it, and they were like, 'What the hell? This isn't right!' So the tour was actually a plan that we all came up with together. We knew that their live show is their strength. Basically the idea was to blow Blink-182 off the stage every night."[31] So, although even agree-ing to the tour in the first place involved swallowing some pride, Green Day rolled out the pyro effects and their full back catalog, and reviews from the time suggest that they did succeed in upstaging the potty-mouthed younger band, whose shtick lacked the driving force that Green Day brought to even their silliest songs.

The band continued rehashing the past with the release of *Shenanigans*, a collection of B-sides, covers, and rarities. They paid tribute to their influences with covers of "Outsider," by the Ramones; "I Want to Be on TV," by eighties hardcore band, Fang; and the Kinks' "Tired of Waiting for You." Dirnt also got a moment in the spotlight: his lyrics appeared on "Scumbag" and "Ha Ha You're Dead." Critics mostly shrugged, taking the view that Green Day was scraping the bottom of the barrel with some tracks. To promote the album, the band took a three week break after wrapping up the Pop Disaster Tour, and then hopped over to the UK for eight festival dates.

They played massive shows to cheering crowds, but by this time the band was coasting. None of them got along very well at this point, and after cleaning out their closet to release two retrospective albums in a row, all three of them felt restless. After the tour, when Armstrong tried to start writing a new batch of songs, he found himself in a creative rut. Dirnt and Cool felt marginalized, and personal disagreements threatened the band. "Breaking up was an option," Dirnt recalled later, "We were arguing a lot and we were miserable. We needed to shift directions." At the time, none of them were sure that they could make that shift.

NOTES

1. Ben Myers, *Green Day: American Idiots and the New Punk Explosion* (New York: The Disinformation Company, Inc. 2006), 161.
2. Ibid.
3. Doug Small, *Omnibus Press Presents the Story of: Green Day* (New York: Omnibus Press, 2005), 60.
4. Marc Spitz, *Nobody Likes You: Inside the Turbulent Life, Times, and Music of Green Day* (New York: Hyperion, 2006), 140.
5. Myers, 165.
6. Myers, 162-63.
7. Myers, 167.
8. Lawrence Livermore, "*Hit List* Interview with Billie Joe," www.greenday.net/hitlistinterviewbj.html, July 18, 2001 (accessed January 10, 2009).
9. Myers, 165.
10. Ibid.
11. Spitz, 142.
12. Myers, 179.
13. Spitz, 143.
14. Small, 63.

15. Myers, 174.

16. Ibid.

17. Spitz, 143.

18. NME News editors, "Green Day Fire Off Warning to The Other Garden," NME.com, January 17, 2001, http://www.nme.com/news/greenday/6053 (accessed March 13, 2009).

19. Jaan Uhelzski, "Warning: Green Day Have Grown Up . . . A Bit," *Rolling Stone*, October 4, 2000, http://www.rollingstone.com/news/story/5920824/warning_green_day_have_grown_up__a_bit (accessed March 14, 2009).

20. Christopher Walsh, "Bay Area Studios See Hard Times," *Billboard*, November 18, 2000, http://www.allbusiness.com/retail-trade/miscellaneous-retail-retail-stores-not/4598188-1.html (accessed March 14, 2009).

21. *Ibid.*

22. Spitz, 149.

23. Small, 71-72.

24. David Basham, "Go-Go's, Green Day's Billie Joe Pairing On Single," MTV.com, February 12, 2001, http://www.mtv.com/news/articles/1439304/20010212/go.gos.jhtml (accessed March 15, 2009).

25. Corey Moss, "Peers Praise Joey Ramone, The Man And The Musician," MTV.com, April 17, 2001, http://www.mtv.com/news/articles/1442906/20010417/ramone_joey.jhtml (accessed March 15, 2009).

26. Myers, 182.

27. Ibid.

28. Spitz, 147.

29. Small, 73.

30. Jerry Armor, "Blink 182's Hoppus Gives Props To Tour Mates Green Day And Jimmy Eat World," Yahoo! Music, April 27, 2002, http://music.yahoo.com/read/story/12060315 (accessed March 15, 2009).

31. Spitz, 146.

CHAPTER EIGHT

Rebuilding an Album— And a Career

As the band limped back to the studio after an exhausting summer of touring, they felt farther apart than ever. According to Billie Joe Armstrong, all three spent the time after *Warning*'s release "not talking about things, and not wanting to rock the boat."[1] They came to resent each other, but never talked about the way they felt, and the tension built up. Armstrong grew frustrated with Mike Dirnt and Tré Cool's passive-aggressive criticisms of his new songs, and started censoring himself, ditching song ideas out of a misguided fear that they'd be shot down. It would have been easy at this point to call it quits, try out solo careers, anything but face their problems with each other. The fact that they had been friends for so long only made things harder. As Dirnt said, "Not being afraid to fail in front of those closest to you is the most difficult thing in the world. We needed to get to where we could look stupid in front of each other—artistically speaking."[2]

"Before we started this record," Armstrong said, "we had to sit down and really talk about why we should be doing this. I love those guys, but it was like, 'How come everybody treats me like a decent human being except these two guys, who treat me like I'm seventeen?' We had to say, 'Hey, we're grown-ups now, it'd be nice if we treated each other with a bit more respect.' Then we made love."[3] OK, so they still had a teenage sense of humor—but they started trying to act like adults.

Armstrong suggested that they add conversation time to the schedule every week: an approach halfway between the extremes of therapy and rock-star sullenness. "We bared our souls to one another,"[4] Dirnt admitted. And it worked. "Before, Billie would write a song, get stuck, and then say 'F*** it,'" said Cool. "The imaginary Mike and Tré in his head would say, 'That song sucks. Don't waste your time on it.' He stopped doing that and became pretty fearless around me and Mike."[5] Armstrong finally felt he could ask for recognition as the primary songwriter, although he had long held that role, and the other two acknowledged his creative contributions. This must have given him the confidence to ask for more input from Dirnt and Cool, because the band's approach became more collaborative right away. They started messing around with all different genres, looking for a new groove and learning not to overthink things: they tried polka, salsa, new wave, dirty Christmas carols, anything that would make music fun again.

Even as they were working out their feelings within the band, Tré Cool had his own issues: he and his wife, Claudia, decided to get divorced after two and a half years of marriage. He was going through all the proceedings and helping to care for his son, Frankito, while the band was demoing and recording. Dirnt was planning his wedding to his girlfriend of seven years at the same time.

LOSING IT

Green Day's new approach to songwriting paid off in a fresh outburst of creativity, and after four and a half months they made demos of an album's worth of songs that they tentatively titled *Cigarettes and Valentines*. They went so far as to have the album mixed and schedule a summer 2003 release. Then in November of 2002, as official legend has it, the master recordings were stolen out of the studio and never heard again—never even leaked onto the internet. The band was forced to regroup, and developed the songs that made up their next album, *American Idiot*.

This probably isn't the whole story, though. As Studio 880 owner, John Lucasey, stresses, it would have been difficult to get into the studio. "Everybody's f***in' writing that it was taken from here. It was not. I mean they took their drives with them at the time. There

was nothing that was ever stolen from here. There are safes, everything, you know? Surveillance, safes, I mean there's multiple steel
doors that you would have to get through too and stuff."[6] In December 2004, however, *Billboard* reported a slightly different story: "Fans
will also be intrigued to know that prior to the 'Idiot' sessions, an
entire album's worth of finished songs were accidentally erased from
a computer drive."[7]

It's possible that it looked like the songs were stolen at first, and
the band later discovered that they were just mistakenly erased, but
the way Dirnt told the story sounded a little different in his first
interview after recording, published in fall 2004. "We came up with
about sixteen songs that were really good," Dirnt said. "It had been
about six months and these were songs that we had been writing for
a while and songs that we had come up with fresh—and they were
great. But moreover from that process, we came up with three songs
over here [he waves a hand to suggest a new approach] that we
thought were worth chasing. We had the songs and we turned in the
record and me and Billie got together and we started talking, and we
got together with Tré and we just said, 'Those are really good songs
but we've got these over here, so should we wait three or four years to
put out these other songs and chase this thing that we see going on
over here?' So we decided to chase those and postpone things."[8] Here,
it sounds like Green Day had already started on a few of their ideas
for *American Idiot* before *Cigarettes and Valentines* was finished—and
that they made a conscious choice to abandon *Cigarettes and Valentines* and head in a different direction.

From all accounts, *Cigarettes and Valentines* never hit the heights
that Green Day was capable of. Lucasey, one of the few people
besides the band to have heard the tracks, said, "It was cool. It was a
punk album, that's for sure. I think it was pretty hard-hitting stuff.
Yeah. And that's about all I remember about it. It wasn't *American
Idiot*."[9] "We were really pissed," Armstrong said of the loss. "But it
ended up being good because we were readying ourselves to go where
we hadn't gone before."[10]

Armstrong may have been ready to move on, but he didn't know
where he was headed. He jetted off to New York—without the band,
without the family—and spent some time wandering around the city,
thinking about his life, his music, the military attacks on
Afghanistan, the rising tensions with Iraq that looked ready to boil
over into war. He also met up with Jesse Malin, formerly of the punk
band D Generation, who introduced him to Ryan Adams. Adams

and Armstrong spent several alcohol-fueled nights and early mornings jamming in the bare-bones studio in the basement of the East Village bar Hi-Fi. In the end, Adams' drinking wasn't the inspiration Armstrong was looking for, and within about two weeks he headed home. "I drank a lot of red wine, and vodka tonics—I was searching for something," he said later. "I'm not sure it was the most successful trip."[11] The new year marked a low point for him, though: at 1:00 a.m. on January 5, 2003, Armstrong was arrested in Berkeley for drunk driving in his black BMW convertible. He spent the night in jail, never once calling attention to his fame. During this whole unfocused time, his wife Adrienne recalls, "he was really questioning what he was doing. It was scary, because where he had to go to get this record wasn't a place I'm sure I wanted him to be."[12]

When Armstrong came back, he and Dirnt and Cool sat down with their longtime producer, Rob Cavallo, to decide where to go next. "There was definitely a conversation at one point," said Cavallo, "where I looked at the guys and said, 'Tell me the God's honest truth—did you really kill yourselves to make [the lost record]?' And they said 'No.'"[13] Armstrong later described the album to *Spin* as a cross between *Nimrod* and *Warning*, and sounded bored just talking about it. "We were faced with this thing where we'd been a band for so long that we were risking repeating ourselves," Armstrong said in another interview. "And I think with the album that got stolen, we really kind of felt like we were. So we were just like, 'We have to push this further—how are we going to do this?'"[14] They decided to keep writing for three more months and see what new material they could come up with. The band had discovered a fork in the road with *Cigarettes and Valentines*, but only now did they start down the road less traveled.

20/20 VISION

Green Day opened up to each other and started to put every song idea on the table without thinking twice. "We became so f****** creative, we probably could've written a whole record in a day," said Dirnt. "It's arguable that certain records were written in a day. No Green Day records, of course."[15] Purely by coincidence, this was the exact time that a group of strange masked Europeans moved into Studio 880 and cranked out an album in record time. "They were in Studio B," Lucasey laughs. "Dude, all I know is that they had some crazy-ass accents. The Network were really some f***** up, strange people."[16] But they were not Green Day. Both bands made that clear—the Network even posted a video online of a press conference where they raised hell at just the mention of Green Day's name. Reprise Records refused to confirm or deny whether Green Day was the Network when MTV News came calling, and an Adeline Records spokesperson could not confirm the band's identity and claimed never to have met the members. Besides, the Network wasn't even a trio. There were five members: Fink, the band's leader, who raised the cash to record by selling nuclear secrets; Van Gough, a Belgian who lost his nose to frostbite on Mt. Everest; The Snoo, an ex-Mexican wrestler; Captain Underpants, a former Olympic athlete with a stutter; and Z, an Icelandic hitchhiker.

Their album, *Money Money 20/20*, embraced all the good and terrible aspects of eighties new wave with songs like "Hungry Supermodels," "Transistors Gone Wild," and a cover of the Misfits' "Teenagers from Mars." Yet somehow, the members of the Network seemed incapable of writing bad songs. The album was coincidentally released on Adeline Records, the label co-founded by Armstrong, in September 2003, and—again coincidentally—reissued by Green Day's label, Reprise, in the fall of 2004.

The Network played live for the first time at the Key Club in West Hollywood on November 22, 2003, in front of a crowd that included members of No Doubt, filmmaker Vincent Gallo, and *South Park* creators Trey Parker and Matt Stone. Armstrong happened to be in the crowd and told a reporter, "There are a lot of rumors about Green Day being the Network and it is preposterous. The only thing we have in common is we both want death to mediocrity in music today and we are all members of the Church of Lushology."[17] Drummer, The Snoo (who is not Tré Cool), would only say that "sometimes, after band practice, the ringing in my ears tells me jokes. Fink is always complaining about Van Gough's mass cabbage consumption. He orders fifty-pound vats of sauerkraut flown in fresh from Bavaria every week."[18] The Church of Lushology, according to Green Day's current road manager Bill Schneider, is a reaction against Scientology that also tries to recruit celebrities. "They're saying that we're in a toxic world," he explained. "But our philosophy is that we should embrace that and put the toxins in our bodies so that we will be stronger. You know what I mean, so that we'll be able to survive. We're becoming one with the toxins. We're not being hypocritical about it. There's no dead alien souls. Just like, a lot of litter, maybe."

Somehow, the Network's shameless experimentation rubbed off on Green Day. "The Network was about finding a way into discovering who they were gonna be and what they were gonna do on *American Idiot*," Cavallo said. "Allowing themselves that freedom led them to sort of rediscover who they were and what they wanted to do, you know what I mean? It makes things a lot easier."[19] Green Day was standing at a frightening turning point in their career, preparing to follow up on an album that hadn't been a big hit and mulling over some new ideas that would have been risky for any band to attempt. But they managed to find the fun in it and go all out. Not that they had anything to do with the Network's album.

AMERICAN EXPERIMENT

The band planned to meet every day to rehearse and write songs together, but each of them had a lot going on in their lives. One day, Armstrong and Cool both had to skip out on practice—Armstrong to register for the community service hours he had been assigned after his DUI conviction, and Cool to meet with his divorce lawyers. Dirnt complained that he'd be alone in the studio all day, and Armstrong suggested he write a song on his own. He rose to the challenge in a half-joking way: "I decided to write this thirty-second vaudeville song and make it as grandiose as I could," Dirnt said. "Everyone came back to the studio later that day. Billie heard what I wrote and was like, 'Oh, OK. This sounds great; I wanna do one." So then he put one onto it, or connected his song to it and he threw the ball to Tré, Tré connected one."[20] Over the course of about a week, the chain of songs grew to about ten and a half minutes at its longest point, with lyrics about Mike watching TV in the studio by himself and an absurd take on Tré's divorce: "I got a rock 'n' roll band, I got a rock 'n' roll life / I got a rock 'n' roll girlfriend, and another ex-wife." "And this whole arc started happening," said Armstrong, "where something that started out as a joke started becoming more serious. It turned into this nine minute sort of rock-opera thing. So we were like, 'This is what's making us happy—we're laughing, we're having a great time, it's total energy—so we should be doing this!'"[21]

They had been working on a few other songs and ideas alongside the epic collaboration they called "Homecoming," like "Gimme Novacaine," which they weren't sure about recording yet. They put "Homecoming" on a tape with everything else and sent it down to

Cavallo in LA to see what he had to say. "I played it and I called them up and I was freaking out," Cavallo remembered. "This is the greatest thing I've ever heard. I thought it was amazing. I loved it. The 'Homecoming' opera, that was a tipping point really. It was a song that broke the boundaries for punk rock."[22]

That reaction spurred Armstrong on to finish "American Idiot," a song that forcefully examines all the confusion and darkness of its times: mind-numbing reality television, the wars in Iraq and Afghanistan, a proposed constitutional amendment to ban gay marriage, the constant raising of terrorism alerts every time the Bush administration was questioned. It all poured out in unapologetic lyrics: "Well maybe I'm the faggot America / I'm not part of a redneck agenda." To make sure that his bandmates were on board with the radical direction he was taking, he played the song for them early on. "When we were listening to it I was like, 'Does anybody mind if I'm saying that?' And Mike was like, 'You can say anything you want.'"[23]

With everyone on board, they jumped in. The ferocity and conflict in "American Idiot" gave them a direction and a feeling to bring out in all the songs that came after it. "After that song was written, we knew where we had to go," said Cool. "As scary as it was to be at the bottom of a mountain that high, we knew that we had to get to the top of it. We were not gonna settle for any regrets, any feeling that we could have done it better. It was like, here we go!"[24] Nobody can accuse Green Day of having too little ambition. They took on the task of writing the first punk rock opera, although not without some hesitation. "We were so afraid to say that for a long time," said Cool. "We wouldn't define it. We were like, 'Let's just go in and start doing crazy things.'"[25]

Some would say that writing a rock opera is crazy, period. Rock operas like The Who's *Tommy* and David Bowie's *Ziggy Stardust and the Spiders from Mars* first entered pop culture in the late 1960s and early 1970s with often-bombastic music and elaborate lyrics that told a story over the course of the whole album. Some have proved to have timeless appeal, and some were ridiculed from the moment they came out. It's a polarizing form: many people roll their eyes at the whole concept, assuming that any band who writes a rock opera does so out of sheer vanity and an overblown sense of self-importance. Certainly punk bands, who formed in reaction to the bloated stadium rock of the 1970s, had never considered adopting that form. But Green Day didn't see themselves as bound by tradition. They were ready to try something new; they realized they needed to shake things up to make their music worthwhile.

This wasn't the first time Green Day had floated the idea of a punk rock opera. "We'd talked about this years ago; Green Day always wanted to have a Beatles-like arc to their creativity. Billie had said that to me when I signed him way back in '93. So my role was to say, 'Hey, remember how we used to talk about that? So why don't we do a punk rock opera?'"[26] Armstrong had also mentioned while they were writing songs for *Nimrod* that the band had thought about doing a rock opera or a concept album then. When they finally decided they were comfortable with the label "punk rock opera," they went all out. They listened to the obvious albums for ideas—*Tommy*, *Ziggy Stardust*—and the not-so-obvious *West Side Story* and *Rocky Horror Picture Show* musical soundtracks.

COMMUNICATE, NEVER HESITATE

In the studio, Green Day laid out everything that came to mind without self-consciousness. Editing could come later—for now, they had to get their ideas out. There was no self-censorship within the band, and, as a result, Armstrong's lyrics added up to some uncommonly harsh criticism of President George Bush and the direction of the United States. The song "Holiday" went through several changes before Armstrong considered it finished, and one of the last touches really makes the song. "There'd been this big hole in the middle, during the breakdown," Cavallo recalled, "and Billie said, 'I've got this insane idea for the middle of the song, and it's freaking me out. I'm going to do something,' and he told everybody to leave the studio. And then literally, ten minutes later he called us back in and there was the 'Sieg Heil to the president gas man. Bombs away is the punishment . . .' He almost couldn't believe he was saying something so direct. He was not scared as much as he was thinking, 'Can I get away with that?'"[27] That section is a chanted, shouted breakdown that tosses in references from all over, the way an old Gilman Street poster would. "I think about that middle part being like a punk-rock flier, a f*****-up collage," Armstrong said. "It's like Nazi Germany with France and California and the Senate, this apocalyptic way of writing."[28]

There was a real risk in putting these songs out there—after all, country stars the Dixie Chicks had just been boycotted and deluged with hate mail after a comment they made on stage. In early 2003, right around the start of the Iraq war, the Dixie Chicks were touring England and told one audience that they were against the war and were ashamed that President Bush was from their home state of Texas. After that single statement, they saw their concert attendance drop by half in the United States, their CDs were destroyed at rallies, and many radio stations dropped them from playlists. Seeing this, the ever-controversial Madonna uncharacteristically chose to delay the U.S. release of her dark video for "American Life," where she throws a grenade at a Bush look-alike, who catches it and lights a cigar with it.

Even months later, Green Day's friends and business associates feared that Green Day would alienate their fans. A friend, the filmmaker John Roecker, cautioned the band. "When they told me they were gonna call the record *American Idiot*, I was the one who was saying, 'Oh no, you can't.' I was the one who was worried about it," he laughs. "Because when you think about it, we know the song now, but then it was a really f****** bold thing to do."[29]

"We discussed the Dixie Chicks factor because it was reality," said Brian Bumbery, the band's new publicist. "I wasn't too concerned about it, I felt like a lot had changed in America even since then and that people were ready to hear artists take a personal stand through their music again."[30]

Of course, *American Idiot* wasn't just a vehicle for an Iraq war protest or over-the-top rock opera posturing. The songs have the same relatable quality that made "Good Riddance (Time of Your Life)" such a universal hit. The best examples are "Boulevard of Broken Dreams" and "Wake Me Up When September Ends," the first song Armstrong ever wrote about his father dying when he was only ten years old. These two songs were the album's first Top 10 singles, in part because anyone can read personal meaning into their lyrics—they stand alone when taken out of the album's story arc, but also fit inside it.

As the band members slowly began to shape the songs, they put more thought into how each song all fit together. They wanted people to understand how this album fit into Green Day's work, not see it as coming out of nowhere. "You have to keep your sense of humor when you do something like this," said Armstrong, "because you don't want it to sound pretentious. I like *Tommy*, but it's so literal. I didn't want to write, [sings] "Here I am, walking down the stairs, preparing some food."[31] They found the inspiration for their main character in the raw emotion of "American Idiot:" despising the narrow-mindedness of the people and the media who surround you and knowing that there's a better path to take. Like the band members, the "hero" wants to get out of his stifling hometown. "It's about this kid, Jesus of Suburbia," explained Armstrong, "and which side of rebellion he wants to go on, whether it's the side where you follow your beliefs or following a path of self-destruction which could be disguised as rebellion."[32] He has also called Jesus of Suburbia's struggle a choice between rage and love. The self-destructive side is represented by St. Jimmy, described by Armstrong as a dark yet sexy punk rocker like Darby Crash—the singer for the early LA punk band the Germs, who committed suicide at age 22. Jesus of Suburbia falls for Whatshername, a girl who challenges his beliefs and choices and gets him to think about what he's doing—she represents love, while St. Jimmy represents dead-end rage. "Writing [the album] was kind of like writing a script and a score at the same time,"[33] Armstrong said.

With the news out that Green Day was working on a new album, Lookout! Records took the opportunity to release a remastered version of the compilation, *1,039 Smoothed Out Slappy Hours*, which collected the band's first EPs *1,000 Hours* and *Slappy* with their 1990 full-length debut, *39/Smooth*. The remastered compilation came with twenty minutes of video of live performances, handwritten lyrics, and old photos. Once again, Green Day proved they were still a meal ticket for their old label.

LAYING IT DOWN

Once the writing and demoing wrapped up in Oakland, the band went down to LA to lay down the final tracks at Ocean Way Studios in the summer of 2004. By this point, the band had fully converted Cavallo. "I've been doing A&R a long time, and there are always signs that tell you if a record's going to work," he said. "I started to see every sign you could possibly see." The band members formed a tighter unit than they had since their van-touring days, and felt more excited about the new songs than they had in years. Armstrong gave *Rolling Stone* a rare update on what they were up to, talking about their nine-minute epic songs. "You know when you're fifteen years old and you're rocking out in front of the mirror playing air guitar?" he said. "I was trying to get that feeling going."[34] In fact, Armstrong unleashed all of his technical skills when recording the guitar solos for the album, something he'd never felt was really called for on other, more strictly punk rock, albums.

Everyone went all-out on the multipart song "Jesus of Suburbia" and embraced how different it was from past studio sessions. "It's ridiculous how fun it is to be able to do a nine-minute song with all these changes and different time signatures," Tré Cool said "It's almost like putting on different clothes for a day."[35]

The band members recorded all of the songs together in one room, which was unusual for musicians on their level. Normally, everyone would carefully layer their part on top of recordings of the other band members, but this album demanded the raw sound and the extra energy created by putting all three of them in the same room. Besides, at this point they knew the songs so well that they wouldn't have to scrap any takes because of dumb mistakes. "We spent the better part of a year and a half in pre-production; we know the songs, and my sound is dialed," Dirnt said during the recording process. "I go in, I'm not screwing with sounds, I know exactly what I want for each tune, and it's time to play and let's get it. I even know the little nuances I want to hear; the little extra magic in there."[36] Harking back to their punk rock roots, they banged out songs together and captured the same feeling of unity and drive that powered their earliest recordings.

Their restored friendship turned out to be the best thing about the recording process, especially for Dirnt: his wife, who he had married just before starting this album, told him she was leaving him on the day they finished recording. He said afterward that the divorce was "a blessing but just an emotional drain. It was horrible and great. When we mastered the record, I cried through the entire thing."[37] Tré Cool also needed the therapy of getting fully absorbed in the music: while they were in LA, he stopped seeing his shrink and his girlfriend, Torry Castellano ("Donna C" of Lookout! rockers the Donnas). They all admitted to tapping into their inner St. Jimmys during recording, but Armstrong explained away the partying. "It was kind of a conscious effort to have a lack of a conscience," he told *Spin*. "For the first time, we fully accepted the fact that we're rock stars. Not to sound arrogant, but it was like, 'Hey, you're only on this earth once, so you might as well enjoy it.'" Despite the heartbreak and hangovers, they did.

READY FOR THE REACTION

As Green Day brought in session musicians to fill out the songs and add the final touches, they became the first outsiders to hear the songs in full. The band brought in Beck's father, David Hanson, to do the string arrangement for "Redundant"—he liked Dirnt's idea that his bass should function like a cello on the track and had the cello section follow the bassline. Kathleen Hanna stepped in to sing the recurring section between tracks, "Nobody likes you, everybody left you . . ." The singer, known for playing in the riot grrl punk band Bikini Kill and fronting the electro-punk band Le Tigre recorded her part in New York and the track was emailed to the band in LA. "Billie Joe was in the headset and he just gave me total direction," she said. "Like, 'No, do it more like this,' and it was kind of like trying to sing like a female Billie Joe."

Jason White, the band's second tour guitarist, heard the demos around this time and compared them to The Who's theatrical 1967 song "A Quick One (While He's Away)," the first hint of what that band would later do in *Tommy*. When Jason Freese came in to play saxophone on "Homecoming," the band played him "Jesus of Suburbia" to introduce him to the album. "It wasn't even mixed yet," he recalls. "And I just remember sitting there and just going, 'Jesus Christ!' I'd never heard anything like that in my life. I remember the first thing hitting my head was, 'This is either gonna be the biggest thing ever or it's gonna go over everybody's head.' You know what I mean? It was like, there was no middle ground. It wasn't like, this is just another pop song that's gonna go to radio. It was so unbelievable and moving and huge."[38] Whatever the reaction, the record was going to be impossible to ignore.

But the reaction was by no means certain. After all, Green Day hadn't exactly hogged the spotlight with their last couple of albums. Their fan base had shrunk, and they couldn't count on a lot of automatic enthusiasm in the media. Many critics were skeptical of the reports that had leaked out of the studio—understandably, if you think of how a one-sentence description of their punk rock opera might have sounded to someone who didn't know the background. "I remember saying, 'Give me an A or give me an F because I don't want anything in between," Armstrong recalled later, admitting his vulnerability. "I remember drinking a lot in those days just because who knew what was going to happen?"[39] Green Day knew what a risk they were taking, but they also knew it was worth it. They were careful not to show anything short of total confidence before the record came out. "Any time you're doing something that you feel genuinely good about," said Armstrong, "but that also scares the shit out of you at the same time, you're on to something great."[40] They knew they had accomplished something great—the only question now was whether the world would agree.

NOTES

1. Matt Hendrickson, "Green Day and the Palace of Wisdom," *Rolling Stone*, February 24, 2005, 43.
2. Doug Small, *Omnibus Press Presents the Story of: Green Day*, New York: Omnibus Press, 2005, 82.
3. Caryn Ganz, "Intimate Portrait: Billie Joe Armstrong," *Spin* magazine, September 10, 2004, http://spin.com/articles/intimate-portrait-billie-joe-armstrong (accessed March 20, 2009).
4. Hendrickson, 43.
5. Ibid.
6. Marc Spitz, Nobody Likes You: Inside the Turbulent Life, Times, and Music of Green Day, New York: Hyperion, 2006, 153.
7. Jonathan Cohen, "Green Day's 'Idiot' Fueling Banner Year," *Billboard*, December 7, 2004, http://www.billboard.com/bbcom/esearch/article _display.jsp?vnu_content_id=1000732979 (accessed March 29, 2004).
8. Steven Rosen, "Green Day," *Total Guitar Bass Special*, Fall 2004, 25.
9. Spitz, 153.
10. Hendrickson, 43.
11. Ben Myers, *Green Day: American Idiots and the New Punk Explosion*, New York: The Disinformation Company, Inc. 2006, 191.
12. *Ibid.*
13. Alex Pappademas, "Power to the People (With Funny Haircuts)," *Spin*, November 2004, 62.
14. Dan Epstein, "Never Mind the Bollocks, Here's a Rock Opera," *Revolver*, November 2004, 52.
15. Pappademas, 68.
16. Spitz, 154.
17. Spitz, 155.
18. Ibid.
19. Spitz, 156.
20. Spitz, 159.
21. Epstein, 52.
22. Spitz, 160.
23. Epstein, 56.
24. Ibid.
25. Tom Lanham, "A Night at the Opera," *Alternative Press*, October 2004, 120.
26. Ibid.
27. Spitz, 166.

28. John Colapinto, "Working Class Heroes," *Rolling Stone*, November 17, 2005, 54.
29. Spitz, 163.
30. *Ibid.*
31. Ganz, http://spin.com/articles/intimate-portrait-billie-joe-armstrong (accessed March 20, 2009).
32. Victoria Durham, "Green Day: Let the Good Times Roll," *Rock Sound*, March 2005, 51.
33. Myers, 197.
34. Steve Baltin and David Swanson, "In the Studio: Green Day: *American Idiot*," *Rolling Stone*, June 24, 2004, 40.
35. Small, 91.
36. Steven Rosen, "Green Day," *Total Guitar Bass Special*, Fall 2004, 27.
37. Hendrickson, 44.
38. Spitz, 167.
39. Dorian Lynskey, "Viva la Revolution!" *Q* magazine, May 2009, 50.
40. Victoria Durham, "Green Day: Let the Good Times Roll," *Rock Sound*, March 2005, 52-3.

CHAPTER NINE

Idiot Proof

With their new album in the can, Green Day started thinking about how to present the radical new approach of *American Idiot* to their fans. "We wanted to be firing on all cylinders," Billie Joe Armstrong said, "Everything from the aesthetic to the music to the look. Just everything."[1] They went back to artist Chris Bilheimer, who had designed the *Nimrod* and *International Superhits* album covers, to put together a cohesive look for everything from the album cover to the stage backdrops to the T-shirts. Bilheimer pinpointed a line from "She's a Rebel" as his inspiration: "And she's holding on my heart like a hand grenade." He created the blocky, stencil-style logo of an out-stretched hand gripping a heart-shaped grenade, dripping with bold, bright red.

At the same time, the band members took another look at them-selves and decided that the crusty punk look they'd coasted on for years wouldn't cut it now that they had embraced an older, wiser, and more ambitious vision. "They were going to step it up," Jason Freese remembers, "They said, 'We're not gonna wear Hurley shirts onstage anymore. We're gonna wear suits. We're gonna wear nice suits too. We don't want to look like we're eighteen. We don't want to look like every other punk band out there.'"[2] For their sharp, slim black suits, they went to rock's king of fashion, Hedi Slimane, who designed men's clothes for legendary design house Christian Dior. And to make sure they looked as sharp as their suits, they all went on the Zone diet, getting meals delivered to the studio and their hotel rooms. On a slightly boy-band note, Armstrong's hair went to jet black, Mike Dirnt bleached his nearly white, and Tré Cool opted for a realistic brownish red—covering the same colors as their logo. To add back some of the edge and flamboyance, they started wearing black eyeliner—the last rock-star touch they needed.

As they had done with the past couple of albums, Green Day played a few shows before releasing *American Idiot* to warm up the live show and test out the new songs on some unsuspecting fans. They hit Japan and Ireland before knocking it out of the park at the UK's Reading Festival; new album notwithstanding, they closed the festival with a massive sing-along of "Good Riddance (Time of Your Life)."

The last piece of prep work was to create a video for the title track. They met with director Samuel Bayer, who worked on Nirvana's 1991 video for "Smells Like Teen Spirit," and played him several of the songs off the new album to help explain the story line and the message. Bayer recalls, "I thought, this is going to be either the biggest thing that ever hit rock 'n' roll in the last number of years or people are gonna look at this record as a brilliant failure."[3] He pushed to make the video just as much of a departure for the band as the record was, and he succeeded. The stylish but powerful clip, which featured the band playing in front of an upside-down green and white American flag, drove home the lyrics and matched the massive riff.

GRABBING HEADLINES

On September 14, 2004, the single and video for "American Idiot" hit pop culture and exploded. Radio stations went nuts for it, regardless of format: the song took over pop, rock, and modern rock playlists. As the band expected, the words "f***," "redneck," and "faggot" were censored—although the last was used to take a stand alongside the Bay Area's queer community *against* gay-bashing. Even with a few missing pieces, the song's message came across in the band's ferocity and conviction.

A protest song this powerful hadn't hit this hard since the days of Dylan. Coincidentally, 2004 was an election year, and the Democratic presidential candidate, John Kerry, looked like he could use some help against incumbent George W. Bush. He appeared to beat Bush in the debates, but just a few weeks before the election, he was behind again. His campaign had been blasting a lot of Bruce Springsteen, and missing who knows how many eighteen-to-twenty-year-olds with that safe approach. Some organizations did embrace the song as a way of reaching young voters, but Kerry never connected with youth the way that early frontrunner Howard Dean had. Kerry didn't get on the Green Day train until the day before *American Idiot* came out. On September 20, they were both booked on *The Late Show with David Letterman*, and posed for a photo op together, but even then it seemed like too little, too late, thanks to the slow-moving machinery of the political campaign. At least the appearance on Letterman helped the band, even if it didn't do much for the candidate.

The next day, September 21, *American Idiot* debuted at Number 1 on the Billboard 200: a first for Green Day. It also topped the charts in Australia, Canada, Japan, and the UK, not to mention Apple's iTunes online music store. Although they believed in the band, Reprise Records was shocked to see a veteran act with slipping sales leap back into the mainstream. "I have nothing to compare it to," said Phil Costello, senior VP of promotion. "This never, ever happens."[4]

"Ten years after *Dookie*, it's just that much more sweet,"[5] Armstrong said, completely unashamed of the fact that big sales meant Green Day's message reached big crowds. Finally, the band had skyrocketing popularity at a time in their lives when they were ready to enjoy it. All the second-guessing and defensiveness of the *Dookie* years was swept away. As the album collected rave reviews from fanzines and national publications, the band gave confident, passionate interviews explaining their vision for the music. "We still wanted to make this record sound like a Green Day record, instead of writing these huge pieces that sort of go nowhere," Armstrong told MTV. "It still has the quality of a record like *Dookie* or *Nimrod*, where it's short-attention-span theater, but we brought it up to a new level for us."[6] The oxymoronic idea of a punk rock opera went down easy with most fans despite the insiders' hesitation early on.

Of course, this being Green Day, some punk purists rushed to denounce the album: they accused the band of leaving punk rock behind (again) while still claiming the subculture's hard edges and leftist politics. But purist punk can be dull, fossilized stuff, more concerned with what you can't do than what's possible. "That's the problem with the punk-rock scene," Armstrong said. "Or at least a part of it: they're afraid of being ambitious. There's no reason why you can't grow, and there's no reason why you can't make a concept record. A lot of punk records are kind of concept records, anyway. *Never Mind the Bollocks* or *London Calling*, those records can be looked at as being completely conceptual."[7] Even though the original 1970s punks were rebelling against bloated stadium rock and self-indulgent musicians who spent millions on terrible concept albums, Green Day dared to suggest that punk could be flexible, and even popular.

TAKE ME HOME, COUNTRY ROADS

As Green Day toured to support *American Idiot* and spoke out against President George W. Bush's re-election campaign, their old friend Fat Mike of NOFX was leading a charge of his own through punkvoter.com, releasing two *Rock Against Bush* CDs that sold a combined total of more than 500,000 copies. The point was not to promote punk, but to take down Bush by registering more young, progressive voters. Unfortunately, though, it didn't work. "We did our job. The youth vote percentage was up more than any other vote," Fat Mike said. "But so was the homophobic Christian vote. They all came out too."[8] Bush was re-elected by an even wider margin than his first victory in 2000. The good news? Punk rockers had become political again—especially Billie Joe Armstrong.

With a new fire in their bellies, Green Day rolled out on the next leg of its monumental tour in the spring of 2005. The band matched the stage pyrotechnics with their increasingly fiery rhetoric: Armstrong introduced songs with lines like "This next song is a big f*** you to George W. Bush," and "I want you to scream this next one so loud that every redneck in America hears you!" He sang "American Idiot" wearing a Bush mask. As they traveled through conservative states, he turned it up even further. The band didn't promote the Democratic agenda or bash the United States so much as it opposed the Bush administration's erosion of civil liberties. "It's obviously not an anti-American record," said Dirnt. "One of the most American things you can do is voice your opinion, and if you see something's wrong, you should speak up."[9] Armstrong pushed the idea of thinking for yourself, ending many shows by emphasizing to the people in the crowd that they are the ones with the power; they elect their own leaders. Tré Cool added a note of optimism: "I reckon eventually all these old f***** who vote for Bush are going to die off and then the younger, cooler generation will vote accordingly."[10] Luckily, they weren't trying to sell albums to the older crowd.

EXPANDING THE BASE

Toward the end of the year, Green Day learned that *American Idiot* had been nominated for two Grammys: album of the year and best rock album. The title track was up for four awards: record of the year, best rock performance by a group, best rock song, and best short-form music video. "The day we heard about the nominations we were playing the Hard Rock in Las Vegas," Armstrong recalled. "I put this pair of green and purple star-covered underwear over my pants. When I walked in everyone was like, 'Why are you wearing that?' I was like, 'I got six Grammy nominations. I can wear whatever the hell I want.'"[11] The band celebrated the beginning of 2005 at MTV's Iced Out New Year's Eve concert, alongside such incongruous pop and hip-hop acts as Lindsay Lohan and Snoop Dogg. Soon after, Green Day had more cause to celebrate when *American Idiot* reclaimed the number one spot from Eminem, three months after its chart-topping debut.

The band took the party to Europe in January: Germany, then Holland, Italy, Spain, France, and finally the UK, where the band's multiple dates each sold out in a single day. The tour helped push the album into the top ten all over Europe. Even though the band was playing huger and huger venues, Green Day kept the bond with its fans tight, continuing their tradition of pulling kids out of the crowd to cover Operation Ivy's "Knowledge." It's one thing to dream about it, but another thing to be up there for real, as one fan found out at the January 25 show in London: he got up on stage, looked out at the thousands of people, and threw up right there. At its fourth sold-out show in London, the band decided to play *American Idiot* straight through, to the delight of the crowd, who nearly out-sang Armstrong. The band had said all along that its music was meant to be heard live, and that this album in particular should have people on their feet—this massive tour was quickly proving them right.

When Green Day got home, the bandmates didn't have much time in the Bay Area before heading to LA for the Grammys on February 15. Green Day dominated the best rock album category, beating out Elvis Costello, but lost record of the year and album of the year to the recently deceased legend Ray Charles. Still, Green Day was the first punk band to receive a nomination for best album. U2's "Vertigo" beat out "American Idiot" for the other three awards. In the following weeks, the band cleaned up at the MTV Video Music Awards, the California Music Awards, and the Kids' Choice Awards. They showed up for all their awards sharply dressed in suits and eyeliner, happy to accept the awards and the applause. It looked like the band members had finally gotten over the inner conflict caused by *Dookie*'s surprise success. "The first time we were the biggest band on the planet, it kind of happened by accident," Cool told *Entertainment Weekly.* "We had been told, and it had been proved many times, that you can't sell punk rock and there will never be a big punk rock record. We blew that myth out of the water."[12] No longer were the group members questioning the validity of their ambitions, debating within themselves if they should reject their fame or make a push to sell more records. They had tried something that sounded impossible just because it felt right—and there was more than a little risk involved. The rock opera format certainly attracted more attention than another album of three-minute songs ever could have. Had *American Idiot* fallen short, it would have been ridiculed, not ignored. But Green Day had succeeded, and all the institutions of the entertainment industry validated them: the record sales charts, the national magazines, the awards shows. "It was the first time ever that anyone was saying very nice things about us," Armstrong recalled later. "And that was strangely confusing."[13]

Its fans, new and old, fueled the whole ride to the top. Green Day got the chance to pay them back in a small way in March 2005: A nine-year-old fan from Wales named Corey George was lying in a coma after a car accident, but after his mother played him *American Idiot* for an hour, he awoke and began to recover. The incident proved the literal truth of the band's message—as Marc Spitz put it, "Really good punk rock can indeed save one from a life of pain and suffering. It saved Green Day, and in turn, it saved their fans, both comatose and otherwise."[14]

Green Day was by no means done reaching out to fans, though. The spring and summer tour took on the feeling of a triumphal march, as the band headed off to Australia and Japan before returning to the United States in April. Green Day spent one month on native soil before hitting up the European summer festivals. The band also booked two nights at the Milton Keynes National Bowl in the UK—not a festival, just a Green Day show. The 65,000-seat stadium sold out for both nights, making these shows the biggest of

Green Day's career, and the biggest punk shows to date in the UK. When the band members returned to the United States in the fall, they lined up more stadium shows at New Jersey's Giants Stadium, San Francisco's SBC Park, and The Home Depot Center in LA. They entered the ranks of elite acts like U2, the Rolling Stones, Metallica, and just a few others who had the massive fan bases to pull it off. "We want to be the biggest band in the world,"[15] Armstrong said without apology, adding that playing live is the true stamp of approval. To those who (yet again) questioned Green Day's credibility, he answered, "Punk sometimes has this defeatist attitude where you can't expand. I look at a band like U2 that started out more or less as a punk band but kept expanding and wound up being one of the biggest bands in the world. And I think it's okay to want that."[16] They wanted it, and they got it: their 2005 tour landed at number ten in *Billboard*'s list of top-earning tours for the year.

American Idiot continued to expand and spawn other releases for more than a year, starting with the title track and continuing with the single "Boulevard of Broken Dreams," which won six MTV Video Music Awards, sat atop both the Mainstream Rock and Modern Rock *Billboard* charts for months, and won the band another Grammy in 2006, in the prestigious record of the year category. "Holiday" also topped the Mainstream Rock and Modern Rock charts after its May 7 release, with its more raucous punk sound. The final single, "Jesus of Suburbia," went out with a whimper, not a bang, upon its October 2005 release.

That summer, "Wake Me Up When September Ends" boasted the most controversial video of the year, with some speculating that it wouldn't even be released in the United States. The video was the band's strongest anti-war statement yet: in it, a young man decides to leave his girlfriend and join the Army. He's sent to Iraq, where he watches, helpless, as the soldiers around him are wounded and killed in the fighting. Director Samuel Bayer came up with the concept for the war-themed video even though Armstrong originally wrote the song about his father's death. "I didn't do it to be political," Bayer told *Rolling Stone* when the video was released. "I did it to be emotional. I find it extremely tragic that eighteen-year-old kids with their whole lives ahead of them are joining the military and seeing horrors that, even if they survive this, they may never get over."[17] Still, there's an undeniably political aspect to the video, and to Bayer's inspiration. Tré Cool told *Rolling Stone* that fall that Bayer had asked a group of soldiers what made them join the military, and the vast majority of them told him that a commercial had influenced their decision. So Bayer decided to use the government's tactics against them and create some strong imagery for the other side. The video topped the voting on Total Request Live, an MTV show where teenagers vote for their favorite videos, proving that the imagery did get through to its "target audience." Its emotional side rang true for teenagers and older viewers as well. Cool showed his family the video without telling them the storyline. "As soon as it came to the part where the guy comes out of the bus and [the drill sergeant] yells at him, my mom's like 'Oh, my God,'" Cool recalled. "My whole family was teary-eyed. She lived through that. She waited for my dad."[18] And although it might seem like Cool had a special right to criticize military recruiting because of his family's experience, the band agreed that any American could and should speak out in the same way.

LOOKING FORWARD

As their ambitions continued to climb, the band started talking about turning *American Idiot* into a movie, mentioning talks with writers in several interviews. The only film that came out of all this, though, was the DVD *Bullet in a Bible*, which immortalized the Milton Keynes shows in the band's first live DVD. The band showcases the best of the new material and its back catalog, including cover gems like Queen's "We Are the Champions." The DVD also discusses the making of *American Idiot* and follows the band members around London as they prep for the biggest shows of their lives. It ruled the *Billboard* DVD chart for several weeks, and peaked at number eight on the Top 200 overall chart.

Even as the band started down new paths in every aspect of their career, old problems cropped up again. Some punks complained that Green Day had betrayed its roots yet again when the band took back the rights and the master recordings to its first albums from Berkeley's Lookout! Records. By August 2005, the independent label admitted that it had fallen far behind on royalty payments to the band. "This is a huge band, and we are a very small independent label," said label president Chris Appelgren. "While that can be very beneficial for record sales, it can also be a tremendous challenge." The label had to lay off six of its nine employees, and many punk fans accused Green Day of killing off one of the mainstays of East Bay punk rock.

Lookout! survived the loss, although two of their biggest acts, Ted Leo + the Pharmacists and Mary Timony, left the label. Green Day wasn't the only band to pull the rights to its albums, either: five other bands decamped around the same time, including Gilman stalwarts Screeching Weasel. "I feel very bad about that whole business," said label founder Lawrence Livermore. "I do feel that Green Day didn't have much choice in the matter; they couldn't go on indefinitely putting up with not being paid, or at least I don't see any reason why they should have to. By not paying the bands on time, Lookout! violated one of the most fundamental principles it has always operated by. It's hard to have sympathy about anything that happened as a result of that."[19] The question of whether Green Day was truly punk rock seemed more unfair this time: had the band stayed with Lookout!, it would have lost money it had honestly earned and allowed a record label (albeit a small one) to exploit it.

The band members took a flexible—and healthy—view of punk rock, anyway: for the band, it meant having the freedom just to be Green Day. "For me punk has always been about doing things your own way," Armstrong said. "What it represents for me is an ultimate freedom and sense of individuality. Which basically becomes a metaphor for life and the way you want to live it. So as far as Green Day is concerned, I really want the band to form into its own thing and not just try to represent all of what punk rock is, because you then alienate people and you also alienate yourself. It's about remaining passionate in punk rock but at the same time just really doing your own thing so it's not just about writing punk rock music, but writing Green Day music."[20] Early on, the band members needed the support of the punk rock community and found something to strive for in that world, outside the typical work and school pressures of "the real world." But as the band outgrew that community, in an often-painful process, it found itself to be an important part of the larger community of music, and the leaders of its own community of fans.

Secure in their rock stardom, Green Day wrapped up the biggest tour of their lives, accepted the lingering Grammy for "Boulevard of Broken Dreams," and prepared to go back into their songwriting cocoon. A lot had happened as they spread their message of free thought and rebellion, most notably the mass destruction in New Orleans when Hurricane Katrina hit in August 2005. Nearly every levee broke, and the Gulf of Mexico came rushing into the low-lying neighborhoods of the city. People were stranded without food and water for days, and many blamed the Bush administration for neglecting problems that affected a largely poor, black population without high-level connections. In a December 2005 interview, Armstrong reflected on life off the road: "It's kind of sad because we're not going to be playing those songs for a long time, but at the same time—especially politically—you want to be more aware of what's going on. So right now, I need a home base to follow up on what's going on in the world and what's going on at home. *American Idiot* seemed like it kept making sense in a lot of ways—from Hurricane Katrina to this new CIA-leak case [when officials allegedly leaked the identity of a CIA agent to punish her husband for opposing Bush]. But it's time to hunker down and take a look at the world around you a little bit more instead of feeling like you're being self-absorbed."[21]

Armstrong admitted his nervousness at finishing up the album cycle and wondering what would come next, but said that this was always the scariest part of being in a band. "We'll start with silence," he said, "and that's how we'll be able to find the inspiration to find another record."[22] The band refused to set a date for new material or side projects, but remained confident that something good would come up next. "We set ourselves up to create an environment with this album that was energetic," Dirnt said. "Where that leaves us for the next record is with a formula that tells us how to set ourselves up in a really good creative way. Maybe it won't work next time, maybe it will, but we'll definitely have an approach." Whatever they came up with next, they knew they had a solid foundation in their fans—and a lot to live up to.

NOTES

1. Marc Spitz, *Nobody Likes You: Inside the Turbulent Life, Times, and Music of Green Day* (New York: Hyperion, 2006), 169.
2. Spitz, 170.
3. Spitz, 171.
4. Alex Pappademas, "Power to the People (With Funny Haircuts)," *Spin*, November 2004, 65.
5. Jenny Eliscu, "Green Day's *Idiot* Hits Big," *Rolling Stone*, October 28, 2004, 21.
6. Corey Moss, "Anatomy of a Punk Opera," MTV.com, September 13, 2004, http://www.mtv.com/bands/g/green_day/news_feature_040913 (accessed April 19, 2009).

7. Dan Epstein, "Never Mind the Bollocks, Here's a Rock Opera," *Revolver*, November 2004, 55.

8. Spitz, 174.

9. Epstein, 56.

10. Doug Small, *Omnibus Press Presents the Story of: Green Day*, New York: Omnibus Press, 2005, 96.

11. Small, 97.

12. Tom Sinclair, "Jolly Green Giants: How Green Day saved rock—and their own career," *Entertainment Weekly*, February 11, 2005, http://www.ew.com/ew/article/0,,1023905,00.html (accessed April 5, 2009).

13. Cairns, Dan. "Green Day return bigger and better." *The Times of London*, April 26, 2009, http://entertainment.timesonline.co.uk/tol/arts_and_entertainment/music/article6154388.ece (accessed April 27, 2009).

14. Spitz, 178.

15. *Rolling Stone* editors, "Green Day Go Big," *Rolling Stone*, May 5, 2005, 14.

16. Sinclair, http://www.ew.com/ew/article/0,,1023905,00.html.

17. Steve Knopper, "Green Day Go to War," *Rolling Stone*, Sept. 8, 2005, 34.

18. John Colapinto, "Working Class Heroes," *Rolling Stone*, November 17, 2005, 54.

19. Spitz, 180.

20. Spitz, 181-2.

21. Colapinto, John. "Billie Joe Armstrong: Rock's Rude Boy." *Rolling Stone*, December 29, 2005–January 12, 2006, 80.

22. Newman, Melinda. "Green Day Starting with Silence on New CD." *Billboard*, January 3, 2006, http://www.billboard.com/bbcom/esearch/article_display.jsp?vnu_content_id=1001772671 (accessed April 26, 2009).

CHAPTER TEN

Worth the Fight

Still slightly overwhelmed by *American Idiot*'s runaway success, and buzzing from the longest tour of their lives, the members of Green Day jumped back into the studio in January 2006 to piece together some ideas for new songs. "We didn't take a break; we started punching the clock immediately," Mike Dirnt said, "We just really tried throwing everything against the wall that would stick."[1] The band felt that they couldn't slow down, but they drove themselves a little crazy by trying to jump right back into their process. "We'd collected so much of people's sweat and vomit and beer from the tour before that we were all so sick. When we started this, I was walking pneumonia,"[2] Tré Cool said upon the album's release. "We probably could have beat ourselves up a little bit less than we did, looking back on it," Billie Joe Armstrong said.

The band members did put their new album aside for a while and switched their focus to the social problems that they hadn't had time to speak about (or even think about) on tour. In February, the night before the band won the Grammy for "Boulevard of Broken Dreams," Green Day and U2 sat down together for a long, wine-soaked dinner at the Chateau Marmont hotel in Hollywood. As the night wore on, they tossed around ideas for doing music together. "We just felt that these were some great people—the way their values were was so similar to ours," said U2 guitarist The Edge. The idea percolated until mid-September, when the two powerhouse bands met up at the legendary

Abbey Road Studios in London to record a single to benefit victims of Hurricane Katrina, many of whom were still waiting for government help nearly a year after the storm. The Edge set it all up through Music Rising, the charity he started after the hurricane, and brought in U2's current producer, Rick Rubin. Over the course of three days in Studio Two (the Beatles' favorite room), they put together a cover of "The Saints Are Coming" by Scottish punks the Skids. "It was almost a punk rock recording in a lot of ways. We just pretty much banged it out," Armstrong said. "To be sitting there in the studio with U2 and talking on a creative level was something you wouldn't imagine in your wildest dreams."4 The two bands debuted the song on stage together with local musicians on September 25, the day the Superdome reopened for the New Orleans Saints' first NFL home game since the hurricane. The four-song set was broadcast on ESPN's *Monday Night Football* pre-game show and included one Green Day song ("Wake Me Up When September Ends"), "House of the Rising Sun," which is set in New Orleans, "The Saints Are Coming," and one U2 song, "Beautiful Day." The single, released in late October, peaked at number 51 on the U.S. charts and garnered one Grammy nomination.

After that, Armstrong clearly felt the influence of U2's lead singer, Bono, and later even wrote his entry on *Rolling Stone*'s list of the 100 greatest singers of all time. Following Bono's lead, (he has put his fame behind a number of humanitarian causes), Green Day branched out into a couple of other projects, including a partnership with the Natural Resources Defense Council. They created a Web site with the environmental organization that included videos by the band and Adrienne Armstrong, tips for individuals to conserve energy, information on current issues, and ways to voice concerns to leaders, including text message campaigns to reach Green Day's youthful fan base.

The whole Armstrong family and a group of friends went down to New Orleans later, in the spring of 2007, to help rebuild a water-damaged house for a local woman and her young daughter. "Towards the end of the day as we were nearing the finish of the front, I suddenly had a rush of emotion," Adrienne Armstrong wrote on the Green Day blog. "I felt so connected to this work we are doing. Working with our hands, sweating in the sun and helping to provide a place to call home for this special woman and her daughter."5 They worked with Habitat for Humanity and Americorps volunteers, and recommended the experience to anyone after their tour of duty ended.

The only Green Day–focused event for the winter of 2006 was the reissue of the band's Lookout! albums on Reprise, but because that didn't require any real promo appearances or touring by the band, they had plenty of personal time. Tré Cool went to Cuba to study Latin percussion—somehow he got around the government restrictions on travel to the Communist island. Dirnt went to Japan and Europe before putting his own house in order: he regained custody of his twelve-year-old daughter, Estelle Desiree in the summer of 2007. His fiancée, Brittney Cade, got pregnant that year, and his son Brixton Michael was born on October 11, 2007.

After actually taking some time away from the band, Armstrong, Dirnt, and Cool were ready to test the waters of recording again. They recorded and produced a cover of "Working Class Hero" for the benefit album *Instant Karma: The Amnesty International Campaign to Save Darfur*. Yoko Ono donated the rights to all of the songs from her husband John Lennon's album *Instant Karma* to help raise awareness of the civil war displacing thousands of people in the Darfur region of Sudan. A wide range of musicians contributed tracks, including U2, Christina Aguilera, Aerosmith, and Ben Harper. On a lighter note, Green Day had a cameo in *The Simpsons Movie* and covered the popular TV show's theme song. You know you've made it when you make a cameo on the show, but the long-awaited blockbuster movie? That's big time.

HOT-BLOODED

That fall, the band started in again on the follow-up to *American Idiot*, piecing together about forty-five songs at Studio 880 in Oakland. They were just as driven as they had been in January 2006, and refused to give in to the idea that they had earned a break and could coast for a while. "*American Idiot* was successful enough that we probably could have mailed in a follow-up," said Armstrong. "And that was reason enough for me to say, 'No, we can't.'" He even taught himself to play the piano, and wrote many of the new song sketches on that instrument instead of the guitar. With a chaotic heap of ideas building up, he found himself still searching for themes. "I want to dig into who I am and what I'm feeling at this moment—which is middle-aged," he told *Rolling Stone* at the time. "We've been doing this for almost twenty years now. You want to make sure you're being honest with yourself. I also have to ask myself, 'What's real out there?' Right now, it seems stagnant."[6]

Holed up in the studio, the band members were starting to feel like they were beating their heads against the wall. They only snapped out of it when a guitar technician showed them an old eight-track Tascam recorder he'd just bought: the eight-track, combined with the garage rock albums they were listening to at the moment, combusted in a night full of cheap wine and quick songwriting. "Me and Billie were just throwing riffs back and forth," said Dirnt. "And next thing you know, we'd written about ten songs after about nine bottles of wine."[7] They put three songs online in December of 2007 under the name Foxboro Hot Tubs, which they later explained was "a place we used to sneak booze and chicks into late at night. But most of the time it was just 'dude soup.'"[8] They released the quick-and-dirty album *Stop Drop and Roll!!!* in the spring of 2008, packed with stomping 1960s-style garage rockers. It got reviewed in a number of big music magazines, and one single made it onto the Billboard Modern Rock charts. Not bad for an "unknown" band—the album was released on Jingletown Records (named for the Oakland neighborhood where Studio 880 is located), and Green Day refused to confirm or deny any connection to the recording. They finally sent an email to MTV News in April 2009, saying, "We think that the only similarity [between the two bands] is that we are the same band."[9]

In May, Foxboro Hot Tubs went on tour, with Jason White, Jason Freese, and Kevin Preston filling out the lineup. "It was, 'Let's just go, rave up, put on funky clothes, wear big stupid sunglasses and throw Pabst Blue Ribbon over ourselves every night for a couple of weeks," said Armstrong. When you see Green Day at their least serious, you know they're about to get serious. Just as they had done with their mysterious one-off band the Network in 2003, the band members used the Hot Tubs as a vehicle to help them clear their minds and get back to their roots in shared humor and small, sweaty shows. They had been missing the physicality of playing live while they were cooped up in the studio, and the tour gave them the jolt of energy they needed to get back to work.

Well, almost. Armstrong's other side project, the long-running Pinhead Gunpowder, also released an album that summer. The EP *West Side Highway* came out on Recess Records in sixteen colors of vinyl—a record collector's dream.

MEN AT WORK

Over the summer, Green Day announced that they wouldn't be working with their longtime producer Rob Cavallo again. They brought in Butch Vig instead, the drummer for Garbage and the producer behind Nirvana's *Nevermind* and key Smashing Pumpkins albums in the '90s. Although he was now an in-house producer for Warner Bros., he'd started out small in the Wisconsin indie scene, so he understood Green Day's roots in the garage.

When he first came in, the band dumped a load of promising ideas at his feet, including several ten-minute "beasts" of jams inspired by the American Idiot sessions. Dirnt estimated they had between seventy and a hundred songs at that point. "Even with all of those ideas, Butch got his head around each one, where it fit," said Cool. "Nothing got swept under the rug or forgotten."[10] Vig pushed the band to go back to songs they were sick of, such as "Horseshoes and Handgrenades," and convinced Armstrong to finish the ballad "Restless Heart Syndrome," which dealt with prescription drug dependence. "Sometimes I think a melody asks something from you that you don't want to necessarily face,"[11] Armstrong said of that song. Rather than trying to change Green Day's style, Vig got deep into their process and encouraged everyone to bounce ideas off each other. "I could feel they sensed there was a lot of pressure," he said. "A lot of times when a band has a big album, they decide, 'Let's go back to our roots and make a quick power-pop punk record, do something really easy.' They didn't want to do that."[12] Armstrong's goal with the songwriting was to rethink the song arrangements and push them out of the realm of automatic rock clichés and the normal way of doing things. "The challenge is to do something that sounds sophisticated but also sounds like you did it all in one breath," he said. Once again, they tried to take what they had learned about reckless energy from punk rock and channel it into new forms.

Over the summer, Vig and the band camped out in the Orange County resort town of Costa Mesa and pieced together the songs that would become their newest album, *21st Century Breakdown*. "We went down to Costa Mesa for summertime, let our families take a vacation, and then we hit the small studio every day,"[13] said Dirnt. With Bruce Springsteen and Ramones records scattered on the floor and front pages from the *Los Angeles Times* tacked to the wall, the band immersed themselves in timeless music and the presidential race between Republican John McCain and Democrat Barack Obama. To shake up their songwriting style, they had two kick drums pinned to the wall as "wheels of fortune," one with different genres and one with different eras—they spun and wrote accordingly. This resulted in a few bizarre mixes ('80s hardcore and '60s psychedelia in the same song), which didn't actually make it to the album, but more often than not it sparked new ideas. Another tactic was to shuffle lyrics around like puzzle pieces. "We were sitting on the floor,"

Cool said. "And Billie had all these lyrics and this big piece of paper, asking, 'What songs go together?'"[14] Whereas Armstrong played the perfectionist, Dirnt strove "for us all to emote one feeling and convey one sound."[15] At times the mixing and matching and second-guessing got to be too much, and more than one guitar was flung across the room in impatience. "This is the album that could have killed us," Armstrong said just before it was released. "It's the most ambitious record we've ever made. We put so much work into it and it made us crazier than any other."[16] Vig agrees, saying, "They were definitely swinging wildly for the stars."[17]

Slowly, connections began to emerge. Two characters appeared over and over: Gloria, a "torchbearer" who's trying to hold on to her youthful idealism, and the self-destructive Christian, who wants to burn everything down. In interviews, Armstrong said that elements of his own personality and his politically-aware wife Adrienne combine in Gloria, while Christian represents the side of Armstrong that he sometimes can't keep under wraps. The story of their struggle doesn't come through as literally as it does for Jesus of Suburbia on *American Idiot*, but it's a uniting thread all through the album. "The characters are just something I sing through. You give them a name and it gives them a life,"[18] said Armstrong. The song "Last of the American Girls" celebrates Gloria, with Armstrong's ultimate compliment: "She won't cooperate." On the other side of things, Armstrong said he wrote "Christian's Inferno" "when I was in the most diabolic state in my head, and vomited out this song."[19] The band also decided to group the songs into three "acts," each with its own highs and lows: "Heroes and Cons," "Charlatans and Saints," and "Horseshoes and Handgrenades." There's no overall plot, but as Armstrong said, "The songs speak to each other in the way the songs on [Springsteen's] *Born to Run* speak to each other. I don't know if you'd call it a concept album, but there's definitely a thread that connects everything."[20]

As the songs came together in rough demo recordings, the band set up a pirate radio transmitter and broadcast its own new songs in between old favorites, both familiar and obscure. It was a kind of test for the new songs, seeing how they fit alongside the band members' heroes. Luckily Rebel Radio never got bootlegged.

CONFIDENCE AND CONFUSION

After their summer of writing, the members of Green Day went back to Ocean Way Studios in LA for the main recording sessions, the same studio where they had recorded *American Idiot*. They rehearsed the finished songs and started laying down different tracks. "I had this 'eureka' moment during rehearsals," said Vig, "where it was like, 'I'm sitting in a room with one of the greatest rock bands in the world, ever, and they are putting the f****** hammer down.' I was trying to be nonchalant, like, 'Yeah, guys, sounds pretty good,' but inside I was like, 'Holy f***, man. I'm a lucky bastard to be sitting here right now.'"[21]

As recording went on, though, Vig noticed that Armstrong seemed reluctant to complete his vocals—in fact, he was avoiding it. "He didn't say anything about it," said Vig. "But realized he didn't want to do any of the vocals till the presidential election. We all had the sense that Obama was going to win, but he might have made some changes if Obama had lost, and the record would be a lot darker than it is."[22] Nearly a year ago, Armstrong had told *Rolling Stone* that he was leaning toward Obama in the primaries, mainly because it looked like former president Bill Clinton's wife Hillary was going to start a Democratic dynasty if Obama couldn't beat her. The thought of simply trading power back and forth between the Bush and the Clinton families freaked him out. Still, he said, "it's a bit early to tell if this is the guy I like. I get sick of the religious-figure thing. People don't question their rulers, these political figures, just as they don't question their ministers and priests."

Politics and religion twist together inextricably in American life, and *21st Century Breakdown* reflected that. The song "East Jesus Nowhere," originally titled "March of the Dogs," lashes out at religious hypocrisy with scathing lyrics like "I want to know who's allowed to breed." Armstrong wrote the song after the band members all attended a dedication ceremony for a friend's baby at a Christian church—he interpreted the minister's words as discouraging people from having their own opinions, and boiled over at the thought that anyone could recommend blind obedience.

But Obama was elected as much for his practicality and even keel as for his transcendent appeal as the country's first black president and an advocate of change. The day after Obama won, Armstrong wrote a new song, "Wonderful." "It was super poppy, sunny, Beach Boys but with fuzzy pop chords," said Vig. "It was great. Hundreds of bands would kill to have this song on the record."[23] Armstrong nixed it, though: he needed to write it at that moment, but it didn't fit with the album's themes of confusion. The hope spread by Obama's election complicated the fighting spirit of *American Idiot* and allowed Green Day the freedom to make their new album more intensely personal, with an even richer and more relatable kind of storytelling. It came just when people were ready to hear it. At the end of 2008, the United States woke up from the election-night party with a terrible economic hangover: the housing market tanked, banks blew up left and right, and people everywhere were starting to lose their jobs. Armstrong described the feel of the album as making out with your girlfriend while the city's burning behind you, essentially the same mix of hope and rage that the country felt at the time.

That was also the exact image they chose for the cover. The art was inspired by a stencil of a kissing couple created by graffiti artist Sixten. Back in 2000, one of the artist's friends snapped a photo of a couple making out at a party in Sweden, and Sixten created his stencil from the photo. "I love their passion, and just had to make a stencil out of it to spread the love,"[24] he said. Green Day hired him to adapt it for their cover, which features a new stencil logo of the band name as well.

BACK IN THE REAL WORLD

Even though the record wasn't entirely finished yet, Reprise started putting the word out in February of 2009. "First listens" in a wide range of national and UK publications announced that *21st Century Breakdown* topped even *American Idiot* in its ambition, but few said it overreached. So far, so good. On March 24, Reprise released Green Day's early Lookout! albums and EPs on 12" vinyl, with *Dookie* coming soon on April 18, and all the other studio albums and compilations to follow at intervals throughout 2009. The vinyl release and early previews were just a small part of the label's grand plan to get the word out on this album in the midst of a recession. The music industry had been declining for years as digital downloads took over from record-store sales, and bands and labels had to get creative to keep making money.

At the end of March, Green Day announced one of the newest ways they were thinking outside the box of the traditional album: they were turning *American Idiot* into a stage musical. Director Michael Mayer discovered their album in the early stages of putting together the musical *Spring Awakening*, which follows teenagers in Germany in the late 1800s as they discover the mental and physical tumult of sexuality—all with a rock and folk soundtrack. After *Spring Awakening* cleaned up at Broadway's Tony Awards in 2007, Mayer approached Green Day about adapting their album for the stage. The band members went to see *Spring Awakening*, and decided that they liked Mayer's slightly anarchic style. In the summer of 2008, the band attended a workshop in New York to test some new orchestrations, and that winter they attended another one to vet the choreography. Finally satisfied that the play could do justice to their album, the band agreed to do the show. They even added some new songs from *21st Century Breakdown*, plus a few songs that haven't made it onto any albums so far. Armstrong and Mayer worked together to flesh out the narrative. When the director couldn't get "Letterbomb" to fit in, Armstrong suggested switching it from a male to a female character, and it clicked. "I thought, 'Oh my God, this guy is so meant to make musicals,'"[25] Mayer said.

Green Day was part of a larger trend as well: musicians ranging from U2 to Bob Dylan to the Scissor Sisters were all working on musical theater collaborations around this same time, in hopes of giving the lagging music and theater industries a boost. Mayer reaped some of the benefits that come with being Green Day when he met up with the band: eating at a steakhouse and drinking plenty of wine, then hanging out at the studio until 3 a.m. while they mixed tracks for the album. "It was one of the great nights of my life,"[26] he said.

The studio, which seemed new and exciting to Mayer, had closed in on Armstrong. All the way into April, he still wasn't ready to let the album go. The record had been mixed, mastered, and mastered again, and it was scheduled for a May release. But in February he insisted on adding another song, "Murder City," to the lineup—based on the uproar in Oakland when a police officer shot an unarmed young black man while arresting him. The label wasn't admitting that they were worried, but they were clearly getting antsy. Eventually Vig had to say something to Armstrong. "He said, 'Okay, now it's time to let this go,'" Armstrong recalled a couple of weeks later. "It has literally driven me crazy. But there is definitely a side of me that loves the chaos."[27]

After all the last-minute tweaking and fussing over the album, it was time to get some air. Green Day surprised its hometown fans with four semi-secret shows in the Bay Area in early April: at the Independent and the DNA Lounge in San Francisco, and the Fox Theater and Uptown in Oakland. (The shows in Oakland were filmed to air later on Myspace.com and as a pay-per-view program for Comcast cable subscribers, so it wasn't simply for the fans.) Members of the press were invited to the Fox, and raved about the band's spitfire energy and complex yet powerful new songs. "We've been deprived of playing live for so long that it was kind of a free-for-all,"

Armstrong said. "It was kind of like playing your first show all over again."[28] He admitted to being terrified of playing a full set of brand new songs, but they got through it with only a few bruises for the accident-prone Dirnt. The band played the entire album at the Fox and then returned for another hour of crowd favorites from past albums and covers like "Shout"—all the while working the stage as hard as you might expect a bunch of teenagers to. "It's funny—we make our most physical album not when we're nineteen but in our mid-thirties,"[29] said Armstrong. It's extremely rare for a band of Green Day's stature to play club shows—much less in its hometown where it could certainly sell out arenas—but Green Day didn't want to forget what it was like to play for a small, dedicated crowd.

Green Day chose the fist-pumping, deceptively simple "Know Your Enemy" as the first single, and it flew to number 1 in alternative rock radio after its April 16 release. "I've never really written a song like that before," said Armstrong. "I've always liked songs like 'Freefalling' by Tom Petty—it's the same riff over and over again. And that's hard to do—firing off on one riff."[30] The lyrics warn against letting down your guard and becoming complacent, and verge on controversial with lines like "Violence is an energy." Armstrong was careful to make a few statements to the press around this time to make it clear that he didn't endorse physical violence. In any case, the song isn't very specific: it's more about having a keen awareness of how society tries to influence us. "He's not on the soapbox," Cool says of Armstrong's lyrics. "He's reaching out to lend a hand, or get a hand."[31] Armstrong agrees: "There's a fine line for me in writing political stuff. It's more about calling it like it is than calling it like I think it should be."[32]

The video had some political undertones, but nothing like the intense narrative of "Wake Me Up When September Ends." On location in downtown LA, the band performs behind concertina wire in an abandoned urban landscape, overshadowed by security cameras and helicopters with spotlights. The huge production (eight cameras, not to mention helicopters) took two days to complete, with the band only there for one long night of filming. Still, like the song itself, all of the prep work and behind-the-scenes action results in a clean, straightforward clip rather than an elaborate reinterpretation. "I had this idea of keeping it simple, of letting the music guide the video, and I didn't know how they'd take it," said director Matthew Cullen. "As it turns out, they were into it. Because despite being one of the hugest bands in the world, they're also one of the most trusting and collaborative. So that made my job *easy*."³³ The video was all about the band's performance, complete with flaming silhouettes at the end, which only whetted fans' appetites for the tour that was sure to follow the album's release.

On May 15, 2009, *21st Century Breakdown* was released worldwide. After the band's long journey back, fans pounced on the new album despite the recession, and it debuted at number one on the Billboard charts. "It's interesting because our country—and the world for that matter—is in the worst shape I've ever seen it," Armstrong said. "But there's this sense of hope that people have. And there's a *lot* of confusion. It's the strangest time. And that's kind of what *21st Century Breakdown* is about."³⁴ Once again, Green Day hit pop culture just when it was needed.

Some minor controversies stirred things up around the release, including the band's refusal to sell a "clean" version of the album—which they saw as censorship—and Wal-Mart's refusal to carry it as a result. "I mean, what does that say to a young kid who's trying to speak his mind making a record for the first time?" Armstrong said. "It's like a game that you have to play. You have to refuse to play it."³⁵ Even without help from the Wal-Mart machine, *21st Century Breakdown* reached fans around the world.

The nineties punks that no one ever expected to grow up had entered a realm that practically didn't even exist anymore: their sound was universal, and their ambition was global. Germany got two preview shows in the first week of May, and the band hopped over to Japan at the end of May to play the MTV Japan Video Music Awards and a small Tokyo show. The U.S. tour kicked off in Seattle on July 3rd (oddly, they played their July 4th show in Vancouver, Canada). The tour dates stretched off to the horizon, with U.S. dates through August, European shows in September, October, and November, and Australia and New Zealand slated for December. Japan, Southeast Asia, and South America will follow in 2010 before a second round of U.S. dates. Armstrong has also said that he hopes to try some new places on this tour, which might even mean crossing the notoriously free speech-shy borders of China. As always, Green Day's goal is to keep building community wherever it goes. "A lot of this record is just trying to come up with answers to the confusion," said Armstrong. "I think if more confused people come together, then hopefully we'll come up with a few more solutions."³⁶ Turning confusion, hope, and ambition into a rallying cry, Green Day is ready for whatever else the 21st century has to throw at it.

NOTES

1. Jon Pareles, "The Morning After 'American Idiot,'" *The New York Times*, May 3, 2009, http://www.nytimes.com/2009/05/03/arts/music/03pare .html?_r=1 (accessed May 3, 2009).
2. Jacqui Swift, "It's our most ambitious album. It drove us crazier than any other," *The Sun*, April 24, 2009, 48.
3. Pareles, http://www.nytimes.com/2009/05/03/arts/music/03pare.html?_r=1 (accessed May 3, 2009).
4. Brian Hiatt, "U2, Green Day Unite," *Rolling Stone*, October 5, 2006, 13.
5. Adrienne Armstrong, "Day 2—New Orleans," http://www.greenday.net/ no.html, April 13, 2007 (accessed May 2, 2009).
6. David Fricke, "Green Day," *Rolling Stone*, October 18, 2007, 24.
7. Pareles, http://www.nytimes.com/2009/05/03/arts/music/03pare.html?_r=1 (accessed May 3, 2009).
8. James Montgomery, "Green Day Exclusive: Yes, They Are Foxboro Hot Tubs, Just In Case There Was Any Doubt," MTV.com, April 10, 2008, http://www.mtv.com/news/articles/1585150/20080410/green_day.jhtm l (accessed May 2, 2009).
9. Ibid.
10. David Fricke, "Green Day Go Bigger on 'American Idiot' Follow-up," *Rolling Stone*, March 5, 2009, 18.
11. Pareles, http://www.nytimes.com/2009/05/03/arts/music/03pare.html?_r=1 (accessed May 3, 2009).
12. Ibid.
13. Mitchell Peters, "Green Day tests new ground on way to "Breakdown," *Billboard*, May 3, 2009, http://ca.reuters.com/article/entertainment-News/idCATRE5422XU20090503?sp=true (accessed May 31, 2009).
14. Dorian Lynskey, "Viva la Revolution!" *Q* magazine, May 2009, 53.
15. Pareles, http://www.nytimes.com/2009/05/03/arts/music/03pare.html?_r=1 (accessed May 3, 2009).
16. Swift, 48.
17. Fricke, 18.
18. Lynskey, 48.
19. Mitchell Peters, "Q&A: Green Day's Punk Opera," *Billboard*, April 30, 2009, http://www.billboard.com/bbcom/feature/q-a-green-day-s-punk-opera-1003968568.story (accessed May 3, 2009).
20. Aaron Burgess, "Heart, Soul, and a Killer Tattoo," *Alternative Press*, January 2009, 84.
21. Ibid.
22. Pareles, http://www.nytimes.com/2009/05/03/arts/music/03pare.html?_r=1 (accessed May 3, 2009).
23. Ibid.

24. NME News editors, "Green Day artist reveals story behind new album cover," NME.com, February 11, 2009, http://www.nme.com/news/green-day/42691 (accessed May 3, 2009).

25. Ellen Gamerman, "Roll Over, Rodgers and Hammerstein," *The Wall Street Journal*, May 1, 2009, W1.

26. Ibid.

27. Dan Cairns, "Green Day return bigger and better," *The Times of London*, April 26, 2009, http://entertainment.timesonline.co.uk/tol/arts_and_entertainment/music/article6154388.ece (accessed April 27, 2009).

28. Peters, http://ca.reuters.com/article/entertainmentNews/idCATRE 5422XU20090503?sp=true (accessed May 31, 2009).

29. Steve Appleford, et al., "Green Day Swing for the Fences on '21st Century Breakdown," *Rolling Stone Spring Music Preview*, March 20, 2009, http://www.rollingstone.com/news/story/26796137/green_day_swings _for_the_fences_on_21st_century_breakdown (accessed May 3, 2009).

30. Swift, 48.

31. Lynskey, 50.

32. Lynskey, 49-50.

33. James Montgomery, "Green Day's 'Know Your Enemy' Video: Exclusive Behind-The-Scenes Footage," MTV.com, http://www.mtv.com/news/articles/1609056/20090410/green_day.jhtml (accessed May 3, 2009).

34. Clark Collis, "Green Day's Billie Joe Armstrong: The Music Mix Interview," *Entertainment Weekly*. April 2, 2009, http://music-mix .ew.com/2009/04/billie-joe-arms.html (accessed May 3, 2009).

35. James Montgomery, "You Won't Find Green Day's *21st Century Breakdown* At Wal-Mart," MTV.com, May 21, 2009, http://www.mtv.com/news/articles/1611970/20090521/green_day.jhtml (accessed May 31, 2009).

36. Burgess, 88.

Discography of LPs and EPs

LPs

39/Smooth

1990, Lookout! Records
This CD has been re-released as *1,039 Smoothed Out Slappy Hours* and contains the songs from the *Slappy* EP and the *1,000 Hours* EP.

1. "At The Library"
2. "Don't Leave Me"
3. "I Was There"
4. "Disappearing Boy"
5. "Green Day"
6. "Going to Pasalacqua"
7. "16"
8. "Road to Acceptance"
9. "Rest"
10. "The Judge's Daughter"
11. "Paper Lanterns"
12. "Why Do You Want Him?"
13. "409 In Your Coffeemaker"
14. "Knowledge"
15. "1,000 Hours"
16. "Dry Ice"

17. "Only Of You"
18. "The One I Want"
19. "I Want To Be Alone"

Kerplunk

1991, Lookout! Records
This CD has been re-released with the songs from the *Sweet Children* EP.
1. "2000 Light Years Away"
2. "One For The Razorbacks"
3. "Welcome To Paradise"
4. "Christie Road"
5. "Private Ale"
6. "Dominated Love Slave"
7. "One Of My Lies"
8. "80"
9. "Android"
10. "No One Knows"
11. "Who Wrote Holden Caulfield?"
12. "Words I Might Have Ate"
13. "Sweet Children"
14. "Best Thing In Town"
15. "Strangeland"
16. "My Generation"

Dookie

1994, Reprise Records
1. "Burnout"
2. "Having a Blast"
3. "Chump"
4. "Longview"
5. "Welcome to Paradise"
6. "Pulling Teeth"
7. "Basket Case"
8. "She"
9. "Sassafras Roots 1"
10. "When I Come Around"
11. "Emenius Sleepus"
12. "Coming Clean"

13. "In The End"
14. "F.O.D."
15. "All By Myself" (hidden track)

Insomniac

1995, Reprise Records
 1. "Armatage Shanks"
 2. "Brat"
 3. "Stuck With Me"
 4. "Geek Stink Breath"
 5. "No Pride"
 6. "Bab's Uvula Who?"
 7. "86"
 8. "The Panic Song"
 9. "Stuart and the Ave."
10. "Brain Stew"
11. "Jaded"
12. "Westbound Sign"
13. "Tight Wad Hill"
14. "Walking Contradiction"

Nimrod

1997, Reprise Records
The Japanese version has the song "Desensitized" on it in addition to
the tracks on the domestic release.
 1. "Nice Guys Finish Last"
 2. "Hitchin' A Ride"
 3. "The Grouch"
 4. "Redundant"
 5. "Scattered"
 6. "All The Time"
 7. "Worry Rock"
 8. "Platypus (I Hate You)"
 9. "Uptight"
10. "Last Ride In"
11. "Jinx"
12. "Haushinka"
13. "Walking Alone"
14. "Reject"

15. "Take Back"
16. "King For A Day"
17. "Good Riddance (Time Of Your Life)"
18. "Prosthetic Head"

Warning

2000, Reprise Records
1. "Warning"
2. "Blood, Sex, and Booze"
3. "Church On Sunday"
4. "Fashion Victim"
5. "Castaway"
6. "Misery"
7. "Deadbeat Holiday"
8. "Hold On"
9. "Jackass"
10. "Waiting"
11. "Minority"
12. "Macy's Day Parade"

International Superhits

2001, Reprise Records
1. "Maria"
2. "Poprocks & Coke"
3. "Longview"
4. "Welcome To Paradise"
5. "Basket Case"
6. "When I Come Around"
7. "She"
8. "J.A.R. (Jason Andrew Relva)"
9. "Geek Stink Breath"
10. "Brain Stew"
11. "Jaded"
12. "Walking Contradiction"
13. "Stuck With Me"
14. "Hitchin' A Ride"
15. "Good Riddance (Time Of Your Life)"
16. "Redundant"

17. "Nice Guys Finish Last"
18. "Minority"
19. "Warning"
20. "Waiting"
21. "Macy's Day Parade"

Shenanigans

2002, Reprise Records
The Japanese version has the song "DUI" on it in addition to the tracks on the domestic release.
1. "Suffocate"
2. "Desensitized"
3. "You Lied"
4. "Outsider"
5. "Don't Wanna Fall in Love"
6. "Espionage" (from *Austin Powers: The Spy Who Shagged Me*)
7. "I Want to Be on TV"
8. "Scumbag"
9. "Tired of Waiting for You"
10. "Sick of Me"
11. "Rotting"
12. "Do Da Da"
13. "On the Wagon"
14. "Ha Ha You're Dead"

American Idiot

Sept 21, 2004, Warner Bros. Records
1. "American Idiot"
2. "Jesus of Suburbia"
3. "Holiday"
4. "Boulevard of Broken Dreams"
5. "Are We The Waiting"
6. "St. Jimmy"
7. "Give Me Novacaine"
8. "She's a Rebel"
9. "Extraordinary Girl"
10. "Letterbomb"
11. "Wake Me Up When September Ends"

12. "Homecoming"
13. "Whatsername"

Bullet In A Bible

CD/DVD November 15, 2005, Warner Bros. Records
1. "American Idiot"
2. "Jesus of Suburbia"
3. "Holiday"
4. "We Are The Waiting"
5. "St. Jimmy"
6. "Longview"
7. "Hitchin' A Ride"
8. "Brain Stew"
9. "Basket Case"
10. "King For A Day/Shout"
11. "Wake Me Up When September Ends"
12. "Minority"
13. "Boulevard of Broken Dreams"
14. "Good Riddance (Time of Your Life)"

21st Century Breakdown

May 15th, 2009, Reprise Records
1. "Song of the Century"
   ACT 1—HEROES AND CONS
2. "21st Century Breakdown"
3. "Know Your Enemy"
4. "¡Viva La Gloria!"
5. "Before the Lobotomy"
6. "Christian's Inferno"
7. "Last Night on Earth"
   ACT 2—CHARLATANS AND SAINTS
8. "East Jesus Nowhere"
9. "Peacemaker"
10. "Last of the American Girls"
11. "Murder City"
12. "¿Viva La Gloria?"
13. "Restless Heart Syndrome"

ACT 3—HORSESHOES AND HANDGRENADES
14. "Horseshoes and Handgrenades"
15. "The Static Age"
16. "21 Guns"
17. "American Eulogy (A. Mass Hysteria / B. Modern World)"
18. "See The Light"

EPs

1,000 Hours

April 1989, Lookout! Records
1. "1,000 Hours"
2. "Dry Ice"
3. "Only of You"
4. "The One I Want"

Sweet Children

1990, Skene! Records
1. "Sweet Children"
2. "Best Thing in Town"
3. "Strangeland"
4. "My Generation"

Slappy

1990, Lookout! Records
This EP has been re-released as part of the compilation album *1,039 Smoothed Out Slappy Hours*.
1. "Paper Lanterns"
2. "Why Do You Want Him"
3. "409 in Your Coffeemaker"
4. "Knowledge"

Awards

1995:

- Grammy Awards: Best Alternative Music Performance (*Dookie*)
- Bay Area Music Awards: Outstanding Album (*Dookie*), Outstanding Bassist, Outstanding Drummer, and Outstanding Group

1998:

- MTV Video Music Awards: Best Alternative Video ("Time Of Your Life (Good Riddance)")

2001:

- *Kerrang!* Awards: Classic Songwriter
- The California Music Awards (formerly the Bay Area Music Awards): Outstanding Album (*Warning*), Outstanding Punk Rock/Ska Album (*Warning*), Outstanding Group, Outstanding Male Vocalist, Outstanding Bassist, Outstanding Drummer, Outstanding Songwriter, and Outstanding Artist/Group

2002:

- California Music Awards: Outstanding Group

2003:

- California Music Awards: Outstanding Group, Artist of the Year, Best Guitarist, and the "Spirit of Rock" award

2004:

- *Kerrang!* Awards: Hall of Fame
- California Music Awards: Most Downloaded Song ("I Fought the Law")
- Spike TV Video Game Award: Best Song in a Video Game ("American Idiot" in *Madden NFL 2005*)

2005:

- Grammy Awards: Best Rock Album (*American Idiot*)
- MTV Video Music Awards: Viewer's Choice Award ("American Idiot"), Video of the Year, Best Group Video, and Best Rock Video ("Boulevard Of Broken Dreams"), Best Direction and Best Cinematography (Samuel Bayer, "Boulevard Of Broken Dreams"), and Best Editing (Tim Royes, "Boulevard Of Broken Dreams")
- mtvU Woodie Awards: Alumni Woodie ("American Idiot")
- Billboard Music Awards: Billboard 200 Album Group of the Year, Pop Group of the Year, Hot 100 Group of the Year, Rock Artist of the Year, Rock Song of the Year ("Boulevard of Broken Dreams"), Modern Rock Artist of the Year
- Nickelodeon Kid's Choice Awards: Favorite Band/Group
- American Music Awards: Favorite Pop/Rock Album (*American Idiot*) and Favorite Alternative Artist
- Juno Awards (Canada): Best International Album of the Year (*American Idiot*)
- MTV Europe Awards: Best Album (*American Idiot*) and Best Rock Group
- Los Premios MTV Latinoamérica: Best International Rock Group
- MTV Australia Video Music Awards: Best Rock Group and Best Rock Video ("American Idiot")

- MuchMusic Video Music Awards (Canada): Favourite International Group
- ShockWaves NME Awards (UK): Best Video ("American Idiot")

2006:

- Grammy Awards: Record of the Year ("Boulevard of Broken Dreams")
- ASCAP Pop Music Awards: Creative Voice Award and Song of the Year ("Boulevard of Broken Dreams")
- Nickelodeon Kids' Choice Awards: Favorite Music Group and Favorite Song ("Wake Me Up When September Ends")
- MTV Video Music Awards Japan: Best Rock Video ("Boulevard of Broken Dreams")
- MTV Asia Awards: Favorite Rock Act
- MTV Australia Video Music Awards: Best Group ("Wake Me Up When September Ends")
- MTV Pilipinas Video Music Awards: Favorite International Video ("Wake Me Up When September Ends")
- Brit Awards: Best International Group and Best International Album
- Amadeus Austrian Music Awards: Best Album (*American Idiot*)
- MuchMusic Video Awards (Canada): Best International Group ("Wake Me Up When September Ends")

2009 Nominations

- *Kerrang!* Awards: Nominated for Best Live Band, Best International Band, Best Single ("Know Your Enemy"), Best Video ("Know Your Enemy"), and Best Album (*21st Century Breakdown*)
- Teen Choice Awards: Nominated for Choice Music: Rock Group, Choice Music: Rock Track ("Know Your Enemy"), Choice Music: Album (*21ˢᵗ Century Breakdown*)
- MuchMusic Awards (Canada): Nominated for International Video of the Year—Group ("Know Your Enemy")
- MTV Video Music Awards: Nominated for Best Rock Video ("21 Guns")
- Nominated for Best Live Act, Best Group, and Best Rock
- mtvU Woodie Awards: Performing Woodie

Further Reading

Appleford, Steve. "An Endless Summer for Green Day." *Los Angeles Times*, September 6, 1994.

Appleford, Steve, et al. "Green Day Swing for the Fences on '21st Century Breakdown.'" *Rolling Stone Spring Music Preview*, March 20, 2009, http://www.rollingstone.com/news/story/26796137/green_day_swings _for_the_fences_on_21st_century_breakdown (accessed May 3, 2009).

Armor, Jerry. "Blink 182's Hoppus Gives Props To Tour Mates Green Day And Jimmy Eat World." Yahoo! Music, April 27, 2002, http:// music.yahoo.com/read/story/12060315 (accessed March 15, 2009).

Armstrong, Adrienne. "Day 2—New Orleans." http://www.greenday.net/ no.html, April 13, 2007 (accessed May 2, 2009).

Azerrad, Michael. *Our Band Could Be Your Life: Scenes from the American Indie Underground 1981-1991*. New York: Back Bay Books, 2002.

Baltin, Steve, and David Swanson. "In the Studio: Green Day: *American Idiot*." *Rolling Stone*, June 24, 2004, 40.

Basham, David. "Go-Go's, Green Day's Billie Joe Pairing On Single." MTV .com, February 12, 2001, http://www.mtv.com/news/articles/1439304/ 20010212/go.gos.jhtml (accessed March 15, 2009).

Brian and David. "Operation Ivy." *Maximumrocknroll*, January 1988.

Burgess, Aaron. "Heart, Soul, and a Killer Tattoo." *Alternative Press*, January 2009, 82.

Cairns, Dan. "Green Day return bigger and better." *The Times of London*, April 26, 2009, http://entertainment.timesonline.co.uk/tol/arts_and _entertainment/music/article6154388.ece (accessed April 27, 2009).

Cohen, Jonathan. "Green Day's 'Idiot' Fueling Banner Year." *Billboard*, December 7, 2004. http://www.billboard.com/bbcom/esearch/article_display.jsp?vnu_content_id=1000732979 (accessed March 29, 2004).

Colapinto, John. "Working Class Heroes." *Rolling Stone*, November 17, 2005, 50.

Colapinto, John. "Billie Joe Armstrong: Rock's Rude Boy." *Rolling Stone*, December 29, 2005–January 12, 2006, 80.

Collis, Clark. "Green Day's Billie Joe Armstrong: The Music Mix Interview." *Entertainment Weekly*. April 2, 2009, http://music-mix.ew.com/2009/04/billie-joe-arms.html (accessed May 3, 2009).

Cometbus, Aaron. "Ten Years at Gilman: A Scrapbook." *Cometbus*: 38 1/2, January 3, 1997.

D'Angelo, Joe. "How Green Day's *Dookie* Fertilized a Punk-Rock Revival." www.mtv.com, September 15, 2004. http://MTV.com/news/articles/1491001/20040915/green_day.jhtml (accessed December 4, 2008).

Durham, Victoria. "Green Day: Let the Good Times Roll." *Rock Sound*, March 2005, 51.

Edge, Brian. *924 Gilman: The Story So Far*. San Francisco: Maximumrocknroll, 2004.

Eliscu, Jenny. "Green Day's *Idiot* Hits Big." *Rolling Stone*, October 28, 2004, 21.

Epstein, Dan. "Never Mind the Bollocks, Here's a Rock Opera." *Revolver*, November 2004, 52.

Farley, Christopher John. "Woodstock Suburb." *Time*, August 22, 1994, http://www.time.com/time/magazine/article/0,9171,981316-1,00.html (accessed March 15, 2009).

Foege, Alec. "Green Day." *Rolling Stone*, December 28, 1995–January 11, 1996.

Fricke, David. "Green Day." *Rolling Stone*, October 18, 2007, 24.

Fricke, David. "Billie Joe Armstrong: The Green Day leader talks Bush, Britney, and being a middle-aged punk for our *Rolling Stone:* 40th anniversary." *Rolling Stone*, November 1, 2007, http://www.rollingstone.com/news/story/17162460/billie_joe_armstrong (accessed May 2, 2009).

Fricke, David. "Green Day Go Bigger on 'American Idiot' Follow-up." *Rolling Stone*, March 5, 2009, 17.

Gamerman, Ellen. "Roll Over, Rodgers and Hammerstein." *The Wall Street Journal*, May 1, 2009, W1.

Ganahl, Jane. "Has Billie Joe Grown Up?" The San Francisco *Examiner*, Sunday, December 14, 1997, section D.

Ganahl, Jane. "Boy's plight unites rival rock bands." The San Francisco *Examiner*, Friday, May 14, 1999, section C.

Ganz, Caryn. "Intimate Portrait: Billie Joe Armstrong." *Spin*, September 10, 2004, http://spin.com/articles/intimate-portrait-billie-joe-armstrong (accessed March 20, 2009).

Garofoli, Joe. "Hard-Core Heaven." *West County Times*, December 27, 1995.

Gold, Jonathan. "The Year Punk Broke." *Spin*, November 1994.

Gordinier, Jeff. "It's Not Easy Being Green Day." *Entertainment Weekly*, June 10, 1994.

"Green Day," *VH1 Behind the Music*, 2002.

Guitar World editors. "Green Day: The Complete History." *Guitar World Presents Guitar Legends*, June 2005.

Hendrickson, Matt. "Green Day and the Palace of Wisdom." *Rolling Stone*, February 24, 2005, 42.

Hiatt, Brian. "U2, Green Day Unite." *Rolling Stone*, October 5, 2006, 13.

Hicks, Tony. "Son's on a roll, but mom's the rock: Green Day frontman's success has not spoiled his mother, who holds family together and—at 75—still loves work as a waitress." *Contra Costa Times*, May 13, 2007, Living section.

Humphrey, Clark. "Kurt Cobain, Seven Years Later." http://www.historylink.org/index.cfm?DisplayPage=output.cfm&File_Id=3263 (accessed December 4, 2008).

Itzikoff, Dave. "Punk CD Is Going Theatrical." *The New York Times*, March 30, 2009, http://www.nytimes.com/2009/03/30/theater/30berk.html (accessed May 3, 2009).

Knopper, Steve. "Green Day Go to War." *Rolling Stone*, Sept. 8, 2005, 34.

Lanham, Tom. "A Night at the Opera." *Alternative Press*, October 2004, 114.

Livermore, Lawrence. "Lawrence Livermore Interview." http://greenday.net/livermore.htm (accessed December 10, 2008).

Lynskey, Dorian. "Viva la Revolution!" *Q* magazine, May 2009, 46.

Marks, Craig. "An American Family." *Spin*, December 1995.

McNett, Gavin. "The Day Punk Died: Tim Yohannon: 1946–1998." Salon.com, April 3, 1998. http://archive.salon.com/music/feature/1998/04/17feature.html (accessed February 16, 2009).

Medick, Fred. "Sweet Adeline: A determinedly small Oakland label proves that punk is still a viable sound." *SF Weekly*, October 04, 2000, http://www.sfweekly.com/2000-10-04/music/sweet-adeline/ (accessed February 16, 2009).

Montgomery, James. "Green Day Mash-Up Leads To Cease-And-Desist Order, Grey Tuesday-Style Protest." MTV.com, December 20, 2005, http://www.mtv.com/news/articles/1518595/20051220/green_day.jhtml?headlines=true# (accessed March 15, 2009).

Montgomery, James. "Green Day Exclusive: Yes, They Are Foxboro Hot Tubs, Just In Case There Was Any Doubt." MTV.com, April 10, 2008, http://www.mtv.com/news/articles/1585150/20080410/green_day.jhtml (accessed May 2, 2009).

Montgomery, James. "Green Day's 'Know Your Enemy' Video: Exclusive

www.mtv.com/news/articles/1609056/20090410/green_day.jhtml (accessed May 3, 2009).

Montgomery, James. "You Won't Find Green Day's *21st Century Breakdown* At Wal-Mart." MTV.com, May 21, 2009, http://www.mtv.com/news/articles/1611970/20090521/green_day.jhtml (accessed May 31, 2009).

Moss, Corey. "Peers Praise Joey Ramone, The Man And The Musician." MTV.com, April 17, 2001, http://www.mtv.com/news/articles/1442906/20010417/ramone_joey.jhtml (accessed March 15, 2009).

Moss, Corey. "Anatomy of a Punk Opera." MTV.com, September 13, 2004, http://www.mtv.com/bands/g/green_day/news_feature_040913 (accessed April 19, 2009).

M. S. Review of *Hectic EP*, by Operation Ivy. *Maximumrocknroll*, January 1988.

MTV News editors. "Green Day/Third Eye Blind Skirmish Results In Skull Fracture, Canceled Concerts." MTV.com, June 22, 1998. http://www.mtv.com/news/articles/1429740/19980622/green_day.jhtml (accessed February 19, 2009).

Mundy, Chris. "Green Daze." *Rolling Stone*, January 26, 1995.

Myers, Ben. *Green Day: American Idiots and the New Punk Explosion.* New York: The Disinformation Company, Inc. 2006.

Nesser, Adrienne. Quoted in "FAQ." www.greenday.net/faq.html (accessed December 10, 2008).

Newman, Melinda. "Green Day Starting with Silence on New CD." *Billboard*, January 3, 2006, http://www.billboard.com/bbcom/esearch/article_display.jsp?vnu_content_id=1001772671 (accessed April 26, 2009).

NME News editors. "Green Day Fire Off Warning to The Other Garden." NME.com, January 17, 2001, http://www.nme.com/news/green-day/6053 (accessed March 13, 2009).

NME News editors. "Green Day artist reveals story behind new album cover." NME.com, February 11, 2009, http://www.nme.com/news/green-day/42691 (accessed May 3, 2009).

Pappademas, Alex. "Power to the People (With Funny Haircuts)." *Spin*, November 2004, 62.

Pareles, Jon. "The Morning After 'American Idiot.'" *The New York Times*, May 3, 2009, http://www.nytimes.com/2009/05/03/arts/music/03pare.html?_r=1 (accessed May 3, 2009).

Peiken, Matt. "Green Day's Tré Cool: Hungry for Drumming." *Modern Drummer*, May 1998.

Percy, Carol. "Project club a place to listen, stomp and celebrate." *West County Times*, March 15, 1988.

Peters, Mitchell. "Q&A: Green Day's Punk Opera." *Billboard*, April 30, 2009, http://www.billboard.com/bbcom/feature/q-a-green-day-s-punk-opera-1003968568.story (accessed May 3, 2009).

Peters, Mitchell. "Green Day tests new ground on way to "Breakdown." *Billboard*, May 3, 2009, http://ca.reuters.com/article/entertainmentNews/idCATRE5422XU20090503?sp=true (accessed May 31, 2009).

Rolling Stone editors. "Green Day Go Big." *Rolling Stone*, May 5, 2005, 14.

Rosen, Steven. "Green Day." *Total Guitar Bass Special*, Fall 2004, 24.

Sinclair, Tom. "Jolly Green Giants: How Green Day saved rock—and their own career." *Entertainment Weekly*, February 11, 2005, http://www.ew.com/ew/article/0,,1023905,00.html (accessed April 5, 2009).

Small, Doug. *Omnibus Press Presents the Story of: Green Day*. New York: Omnibus Press, 2005.

Smith, Tracy. "Green Day Having the Time of Their Lives." CBS.com, May 24, 2009, http://www.cbsnews.com/stories/2009/05/24/sunday/main5037160.shtml (accessed May 31, 2009).

Spitz, Marc. *Nobody Likes You: Inside the Turbulent Life, Times, and Music of Green Day*. New York: Hyperion, 2006.

Srinivasan, Rajesh. "Best Thing In Town: While Green Day Rose to Fame on the Local Gilman Stage, Their Relations with the Venue Soured." *The Daily Californian*, December 1, 2008.

Stout, Gene. "A Message of Love, Grief for Cobain." *The Seattle Post-Intelligencer*, Monday, April 11, 1004, A1.

Swift, Jacqui. "It's our most ambitious album. It drove us crazier than any other." *The Sun*, April 24, 2009, 48.

Uhelszki, Jaan. "It's Not Easy Being Green Day." *San Francisco Chronicle*, Sunday, October 1, 1995, PK-31.

Uhelszki, Jaan. "Pop Quiz: Q&A With Billie Joe Armstrong of Green Day." *San Francisco Chronicle*, Sunday, November 19, 1995, PK-44.

Uhelszki, Jaan. "Green Day Gets Bigwig Manager." *San Francisco Chronicle*, Sunday, July 28, 1996, PK-39.

Uhelszki, Jaan. "Green Day: Still a Bunch of Punks." *San Francisco Chronicle*, Sunday, October 12, 1997, PK-45.

Uhelzski, Jaan. "Warning: Green Day Have Grown Up . . . A Bit." *Rolling Stone*, October 4, 2000, http://www.rollingstone.com/news/story/5920824/warning_green_day_have_grown_up__a_bit (accessed March 14, 2009).

Walsh, Christopher. "Bay Area Studios See Hard Times." *Billboard*, November 18, 2000, http://www.allbusiness.com/retail-trade/miscellaneous-retail-retail-stores-not/4598188-1.html (accessed March 14, 2009).

Wieder, Judy. "Coming Clean: Woodstock '94 star Billie Joe of Green Day goes triple platinum and lines up with the pansies." *The Advocate*, January 24, 1995.

Index

About the Author

Kjersti Egerdahl has edited pop culture books on everything from *Star Wars* to Jane Austen, and most recently worked with former Rolling Stone writer Ben Fong-Torres on his book *Grateful Dead Scrapbook*. During her tenure as West Coast editor of *Performer* magazine in San Francisco, she covered Bay Area and West Coast music of all genres. She has spoken about local music at San Francisco's Noise Pop festival and written for *Paste* and *Flavorpill*, among other publications. Ms. Egerdahl would like to thank Danilo Markov, Murray Bowles, Edwina Hay, and all her supportive friends for their help with this book. She lives in Seattle, and her writing can be found online at www.kjerstiegerdahl.com.